GO! with Microsoft®
Office 2016
Discipline Specific Projects

Shelley Gaskin and Alan Shapiro

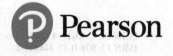

330 Hudson Street, NY, NY 10013

Vice President, Career Skills: Andrew Gilfillan
Executive Editor: Jenifer Niles
Team Lead, Project Management: Laura Burgess
Development Editor: Nancy Lamm
Editorial Assistant: Michael Campbell
Director of Product Marketing: Maggie Waples
Director of Field Marketing: Leigh Ann Sims
Field Marketing Managers: Molly Schmidt and Joanna Conley
Marketing Coordinator: Susan Osterlitz
Operations Specialist: Diane Peirano
Senior Art Director: Diane Ernsberger

Cover Photos: GaudiLab, Rawpixel.com, Pressmaster, Eugenio Marongiu, Boggy, Gajus, Rocketclips, Inc.
Associate Director of Design: Blair Brown
Director of Media Development: Blaine Christine
Media Project Manager, Production: John Cassar
Full-Service Project Management: Amy Kopperude
Composition: iEnergizer Aptara®, Ltd.
Printer/Binder: LSC Communications
Cover Printer: LSC Communications
Text Font: Times LT Pro

Cataloging-in-Publication Data is on file with the Library of Congress.

2 18

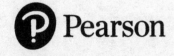

ISBN 10: 0-13-444491-4
ISBN 13: 978-0-13-444491-8

Brief Contents

Chapter 1   Culinary Arts... 1

Chapter 2   Healthcare 35

Chapter 3   Administration of Justice 71

Chapter 4   Legal..105

Appendix A   Proper Business Letter Format.......................A-1

Appendix B   Basic MLA Paper Formatting with
Microsoft Word 2016................................ B-1

Appendix C   Tracking Changes in Word Documents C-1

Index I-1

Table of Contents

Chapter 1 Culinary Arts 1

Word 2016

GO! Make It 2

PROJECT 1A   Culinary Bistro Mailing: Part 1 Culinary Bistro Letter 2

    Part 2 Culinary Bistro Flyer 4

    Part 3 Culinary Bistro Mailing Labels 6

    Part 4 Culinary Bistro Form Letters 8

GO! Think 10

PROJECT 1B   Culinary Gala Mailing: Part 1 Culinary Gala Letter 10

    Part 2 Culinary Gala Flyer 11

    Part 3 Culinary Gala Mailing Labels 12

    Part 4 Culinary Gala Form Letters 13

Excel 2016

GO! Make It 14

PROJECT 1C   Food Costing 14

GO! Think 18

PROJECT 1D   Hudson Grill 18

Access 2016

GO! Make It 20

PROJECT 1E   Recipe Database 20

GO! Think 28

PROJECT 1F   Kitchen Inventory Database 28

PowerPoint 2016

GO! Make It 30

PROJECT 1G   Community Garden Presentation 30

GO! Think 33

PROJECT 1H   Healthy Recipe Presentation 33

Chapter 2 Healthcare 35

Word 2016

GO! Make It 36

PROJECT 2A   Healthcare Dental Mailing: Part 1 Healthcare Dental Letter 36

Part 2 Healthcare Dental Newsletter...38

Part 3 Healthcare Dental Mailing Labels...40

Part 4 Healthcare Dental Form Letters...42

GO! Think   44

PROJECT 2B   Healthcare Medical Mailing: Part 1 Healthcare Medical Letter 44

Part 2 Healthcare MLA Paper..45

Part 3 Healthcare Medical Mailing Labels...47

Part 4 Healthcare Medical Form Letters...48

Excel 2016

GO! Make It   49

PROJECT 2C   Medical Invoice 49

GO! Think   53

PROJECT 2D   Medical Supplies Order 53

Access 2016

GO! Make It   55

PROJECT 2E   Inventory Database 55

GO! Think   65

PROJECT 2F   Billing Database 65

PowerPoint 2016

GO! Make It   67

PROJECT 2G   Lowering Blood Pressure Presentation 67

GO! Think   70

PROJECT 2H   Patient Presentation...70

Chapter 3   Administration of Justice 71

Word 2016

GO! Make It   72

PROJECT 3A   Neighborhood Watch Mailing: Part 1 Neighborhood Watch Letter 72

Part 2 Neighborhood Watch Newsletter..74

Part 3 Neighborhood Watch Mailing Labels...76

Part 4 Neighborhood Watch Form Letters...78

GO! Think   80

PROJECT 3B   Seniors Mailing: Part 1 Seniors Letter 80

Part 2 Seniors Newsletter..81

Part 3 Seniors Mailing Labels...82

Part 4 Seniors Form Letters...83

Excel 2016

GO! Make It 84

PROJECT 3C Police Calls 84

GO! Think 88

PROJECT 3D Parking 88

Access 2016

GO! Make It 90

PROJECT 3E Training Database 90

GO! Think 99

PROJECT 3F Community Policing Database 99

PowerPoint 2016

GO! Make It 100

PROJECT 3G Syber Crime Presentation 100

GO! Think 103

PROJECT 3H Community Presentation 103

Chapter 4 Legal 105

Word 2016

GO! Make It 106

Project 4A Client Mailing: Part 1 Client Letter 106

Part 2 Motion Testimony 108

Part 3 Client Labels 111

Part 4 Client Form Letters 113

GO! Think 115

PROJECT 4B Legal Stock Mailing: Part 1 Stock Letter 115

Part 2 Copyright Law Paper 116

Part 3 Stock Labels 118

Part 4 Stock Form Letters 119

Excel 2016

GO! Make It 120

PROJECT 4C Stockholder Ledger 120

GO! Think 125

PROJECT 4D Billable Hours 125

Access 2016

GO! Make It   127

Project 4E   Caseload Database 127

GO! Think   138

PROJECT 4F   Stockholders Database 138

PowerPoint 2013

GO! Make It   140

PROJECT 4G   Jury Selection 140

GO! Think   144

PROJECT 4H   Community Presentation 144

Appendix A   **Proper Business Letter Format** **A-1**

Appendix B   **Basic MLA Paper Formatting with Microsoft Word 2016** **B-1**

Appendix C   **Tracking Changes in Word Documents** ... **C-1**

Index **I-1**

About the Authors

Shelley Gaskin, Series Editor, is a professor in the Business and Computer Technology Division at Pasadena City College in Pasadena, California. She holds a bachelor's degree in Business Administration from Robert Morris College (Pennsylvania), a master's degree in Business from Northern Illinois University, and a doctorate in Adult and Community Education from Ball State University (Indiana). Before joining Pasadena City College, she spent 12 years in the computer industry, where she was a systems analyst, sales representative, and director of Customer Education with Unisys Corporation. She also worked for Ernst & Young on the development of large systems applications for their clients. She has written and developed training materials for custom systems applications in both the public and private sector, and has also written and edited numerous computer application textbooks.

This book is dedicated to my students, who inspire me every day.

Alan Shapiro worked as an Instructional Designer at St. Petersburg College for 18 years. In this role, he worked with faculty on best practices for using technology in the classroom to increase student success. He was also an Adjunct Instructor for Computer Applications courses. Alan currently works as an IT Implementation Specialist.

This book is dedicated to the success of all students, both those in class with me and those using this book!

Instructor Materials

Student Assignment Tracker (previously called Assignment Sheets) – Lists all the assignments for the chapter. Just add the course information, due dates, and points. Providing these to students ensures they will know what is due and when.

Scripted Lectures – A script to guide your classroom lecture of each instructional project.

PowerPoint Lectures – PowerPoint presentations for each chapter.

Prepared Exams – Exams for each chapter.

Test Bank – Includes a variety of test questions for each chapter.

Student Data Files – www.pearsonhighered.com/go.

Syllabus Template – Outlines various plans for covering the content in different length courses.

Discipline Specific Projects

You will complete the following discipline specific projects:

Word	GO! Make It | Project 1A Culinary Bistro Mailing (p. 2)

Word

GO! Make It | Project 1A Culinary Bistro Mailing (p. 2)

Part 1 Create a proper business letter to match visual summary. Use graphics, text box, no spacing style, and character and paragraph formatting.

Part 2 Create a flyer to match visual summary.
Use graphics, SmartArt, lists, character and paragraph formatting, table, tab stops, footnotes, and save as PDF.

Part 3 Create mailing labels to match visual summary.
Edit table. Use character and paragraph formatting and mail merge.

Part 4 Create form letters to match visual summary.
Edit table. Use mail merge.

GO! Think | Project 1B Culinary Gala Mailing (p. 10)

Part 1 Create a business letter to invite businesses to a fund-raising event.
Use graphics, text box, no spacing style, and character and paragraph formatting.

Part 2 Create a flyer.
Use graphics, SmartArt, lists, character and paragraph formatting, table, tab stops, footnotes, and save as PDF.

Part 3 Create mailing labels.
Edit table. Use character and paragraph formatting and mail merge.

Part 4 Create form letters.
Use mail merge.

Excel

GO! Make It | Project 1C Food Costing (p. 14)

Create a workbook to match visual summary.
Enter data, formulas, and functions; chart data; group worksheets; format; and make summary sheet.

GO! Think | Project 1D Hudson Grill (p. 18)

Create a workbook to analyze monthly restaurant sales.
Enter data, formulas, and functions; chart data; group worksheets; format; and make summary sheet.

Access

GO! Make It | Project 1E Recipe Database (p. 20)

Work with a database to match visual summary. Add table, edit table structure, and join tables; create forms and reports; and create queries with compound criteria, calculated fields, and grouping.

GO! Think | Project 1F Kitchen Inventory Database (p. 28)

Work with a database to track suppliers and inventory data. Add table, edit table structure, and join tables; create forms and reports; and create queries with compound criteria, calculated fields, and grouping.

PowerPoint

GO! Make It | Project 1G Community Garden Presentation (p. 30)

Create a presentation to match visual summary. Format slides and work with pictures, tables, charts, WordArt, SmartArt, animation, transitions, backgrounds, and themes.

GO! Think | Project 1H Healthy Recipe Presentation (p. 33)

Create a presentation about preparing a healthy recipe. Format slides and work with pictures, tables, charts, WordArt, SmartArt, animation, transitions, backgrounds, and themes.

CONTENT-BASED ASSESSMENTS

Apply skills from these objectives:

1 Create a New Document from an Existing Document

2 Change Document and Paragraph Layout

3 Insert and Format Graphics

4 Use Special Character and Paragraph Formatting

5 Change and Reorganize Text

6 Use Proofing Options

7 Insert and Modify Text Boxes and Shapes

8 Preview and Print a Document

GO! Make It Project 1A Culinary Bistro Mailing: Part 1 Culinary Bistro Letter

PROJECT FILES

For Project 1A Culinary Bistro Mailing Part 1, you will need the following files:

w1A_Bistro_Letter
w1A_Bistro_Logo

You will save your document as:

Lastname_Firstname_1A_Bistro_Letter

PROJECT RESULTS

800 West Pikes Peak Avenue
Colorado Springs, CO 80903
(719) 500-1234
www.bistroinabox.com

Bistro in a Box

May 15, 2019

Mr. Jose Santos
1249 Cleveland Drive
Colorado Springs, CO 80903

Dear Mr. Santos:

Subject: Gourmet Box Lunches Available for Delivery

Looking for an excellent caterer to deliver lunch for your next business meeting or training session? Bistro in a Box is happy to announce that we are expanding our business in Colorado Springs. Gourmet box lunches are now available for delivery in your area with a selection that will satisfy everyone—and prices that will make even the bean counters happy!

You may choose to schedule a regular date and time for automatic free delivery right to your office door. Your employees will never want to miss a meeting catered by Bistro in a Box. Take a look at the enclosed order form and then call, fax, or visit our website. We will take care of the rest! I personally guarantee your satisfaction.

Sincerely,

Chef Pete Hudson

Enclosure

Lastname_Firstname_1A_Bistro_Letter

Word 2016, Windows 10, Microsoft Corporation.

FIGURE 1.1 Project 1A, Part 1 Bistro Letter

(Project 1A Part 1 Culinary Bistro Letter continues on the next page)

CONTENT-BASED ASSESSMENTS

1 Create a folder in which to save your files for this project called **Culinary Bistro Mailing**. From the student files that accompany this text, locate and copy the file **w1A_Bistro_Logo** to this folder.

2 From the student files that accompany this text, locate and open the file **w1A_Bistro_Letter**, and then save the file in the **Culinary Bistro Mailing** folder as **Lastname_Firstname_1A_Bistro_Letter**. You will use this file to create a properly formatted business letter to match the one shown in Figure 1.1.

3 Insert a footer with the file name as a Quick Parts field in the footer.

4 Change the top margin to .5". Verify that the side and bottom margins are set to 1".

5 For the entire document, change the line spacing to single, and change the paragraph spacing after to zero. Verify that all indents are set to zero.

6 In the letterhead, from your Bistro Mailing files, insert the picture **w1A_Bistro_Logo**. Resize, wrap text around the logo image, and position it in the letterhead.

7 At the top of the page, enter and align the *Bistro in a Box* text, and format the font to match the letterhead shown in Figure 1.1. Add space before the paragraph if needed.

8 Use a text box for the contact information. Add a top border to the blank line below the letterhead, as shown in Figure 1.1.

9 From the ribbon, insert the current date below the letterhead and above the recipient's address block and choose a date format to match the one shown in Figure 1.1.

10 Make corrections to the text, including size, capitalization, punctuation, and content to match the proper business letter format shown in Figure 1.1.

11 Format the letter by adding and removing blank lines to match the proper vertical spacing shown in Figure 1.1.

12 Correct any spelling and grammar errors. Preview the document and compare it with Figure 1.1, making adjustments as needed.

13 Save and close the document and submit it as directed by your instructor.

CONTENT-BASED ASSESSMENTS

Apply skills from these objectives:

1. Create a New Document from an Existing Document
2. Change Document and Paragraph Layout
3. Insert a SmartArt Graphic
4. Insert Footnote
5. Insert and Format Graphics
6. Use Special Character and Paragraph Formatting
7. Change and Reorganize Text
8. Create and Format a Table
9. Create and Modify Lists
10. Set and Modify Tab Stops
11. Use Proofing Options
12. Preview and Print a Document
13. Save a Document as a PDF

📁 PROJECT FILES

For Project 1A Culinary Bistro Mailing Part 2, you will need the following files:

w1A_Bistro_Flyer
w1A_Bistro_Logo

You will save your documents as:

Lastname_Firstname_1A_Bistro_Flyer
Lastname_Firstname_1A_Bistro_Flyer_PDF

PROJECT RESULTS

Bistro in a Box

Full menu descriptions and online ordering available on our website: www.bistroinabox.com.

Each box lunch includes a fresh fruit salad, chips, cookie of the day, soft drink or bottled water, and eating utensils. All boxes are priced at $9.50 each.[1]

Gourmet Sandwiches	Quantity	Specialty Wraps & Salads	Quantity
Traditional Club Sandwich		Florentine Vegetarian Wrap	
Southwest Chicken Sandwich		Asian Delight Wrap	
Ham and Cheese Favorite Sandwich		Chipotle Beef Wrap	
Very Veggie Sandwich		Ranchero Chicken Wrap	
Tasty Turkey Sandwich		Caesar Salad	
Rancher's BBQ Beef Sandwich		Chicken Caesar Salad	
Italian Hoagie Sandwich		Asian Delight Salad	
Tuna Salad Sandwich		Cobb Salad	
Port Tenderloin Sandwich		Vegetarian Garden Salad	

- 🍽 Free delivery for orders of $30 or more
- 🍽 Same day delivery with four hours advance notice
- 🍽 Open Monday through Friday, 7:00 a.m. to 3:00 p.m.

Call, fax, or visit our website to place your order

Phone 719-555-1234
Fax 719-555-1234
Website .... www.Bistroinabox.com

---
[1] Prices Effective through August 2019

Lastname_Firstname_1A_Bistro_Flyer

Word 2016, Windows 10, Microsoft Corporation.

FIGURE 1.2 Project 1A, Part 2 Bistro Flyer

(Project 1A Part 2 Culinary Bistro Flyer continues on the next page)

CONTENT-BASED ASSESSMENTS

1 From the student files that accompany this text, locate and open the file **w1A_Bistro_Flyer**, and then save the file in the **Culinary Bistro Mailing** folder as **Lastname_Firstname_1A_Bistro_Flyer**. You will use this file to create a one-page flyer that looks like the Bistro Flyer shown in Figure 1.2.

2 Insert a footer with the file name as a Quick Parts field at the right of the footer.

3 Insert and format a table to match the table shown in Figure 1.2.

4 Apply Webding 228 bullets.

5 Insert the **w1A_Bistro_Logo** picture file. Set text wrapping, size, and position.

6 Insert a paragraph border to match Figure 1.2.

7 Insert a SmartArt graphic to match Figure 1.2.

8 Set tab stops, and enter the phone, fax, and website text.

9 At the end of the second paragraph, insert a footnote asterisk. Enter the footnote text as shown in Figure 1.2.

10 Set line spacing, align text, and format fonts to match Figure 1.2.

11 Check the flyer for spelling and grammar errors, and correct any errors you find. Preview the document and compare with Figure 1.2, making adjustments as needed. Ensure the flyer fits on one page.

12 Save the document.

13 Save the document again as a PDF file with the name **Lastname_Firstname_1A_Bistro_Flyer_PDF** in your **Culinary Bistro Mailing** folder. Close the file.

14 Submit file(s) as directed by your instructor.

Apply skills from these objectives:

1. Create Mailing Labels Using Mail Merge
2. Format a Table
3. Change Document and Paragraph Layout
4. Preview and Print a Document

 PROJECT FILES

For Project 1A Culinary Bistro Mailing Part 3, you will need the following files:

New blank Word document

w1A_Bistro_Addresses

You will save your document as:

Lastname_Firstname_1A_Bistro_Labels

PROJECT RESULTS

Firstname Lastname
My College
55555 College Way
College Town, CO 80903

Rebecca Patterson
Colorado Springs City Bank
4321 Cascade Avenue, Suite 200
Colorado Springs, CO 80903

Ernest Aguilar
American Land and Title Co.
50 South Nevada Avenue
Colorado Springs, CO 80903

Audra Blanch
Children's Advocacy Center
9175 Main Street
Security, CO 80911

Natasha Montgomery
Montgomery and Walters, LLC
75 Tejon Street
Colorado Springs, CO 80903

Louis Valdez
Pikes Peak Financial Services
5040 Widefield Avenue
Security, CO 80911

Jen Li Wang
National Mortgage Brokers
900 Hancock Boulevard
Colorado Springs, CO 80909

Warren Turner-Richardson
Majestic View Hotel
100 Pikes Peak Avenue
Colorado Springs, CO 80903

LaKeisha Washington
Mountain States Energy
39875 Blaney Road
Fountain, CO 80817

Adam Meiklejohn
Network Solutions, Inc.
222 East Airport Road
Colorado Springs, CO 80909

Carter Smith
El Paso County Utilities
87654 Santa Fe Drive
Fountain, CO 80817

Lastname_Firstname_1A_Bistro_Labels

FIGURE 1.3 Project 1A, Part 3 Bistro Mailing Labels

(Project 1A Part 3 Culinary Bistro Mailing Labels continues on the next page)

CONTENT-BASED ASSESSMENTS

1 From the student files that accompany this text, locate and open the file **w1A_Bistro_Addresses**, and add yourself to the top of the mailing list. Save the file in the **Culinary Bistro Mailing** folder as **Lastname_Firstname_1A_Bistro_Addresses**, and close the file.

2 Starting with a new blank Word document, use mail merge to create a labels document that looks like the Bistro mailing labels shown in Figure 1.3. Save this file as **Lastname_Firstname_1A_Bistro_Label_Main** in your **Culinary Bistro Mailing** folder so you do not confuse it with your final results file.

3 Your labels are Avery US Letter, 5160 Easy Peel Address labels, which are 1" tall by 2.63" wide.

4 Use **Lastname_Firstname_1A_Bistro_Addresses** as the recipient data source.

5 Ensure that all lines fit in the label area. Preview the document and compare with Figure 1.3, making adjustments as needed. Save the main document.

6 At the end of the merge, *Edit individual labels* to create a new file with only the label text. Save your new address labels document in your **Culinary Bistro Mailing** folder as **Lastname_Firstname_1A_Bistro_Labels**.

7 To the footer add the file name as a Quick Parts field. Preview the document and if necessary, delete blank lines or row(s) at the bottom of the table so that the entire document fits on one page (even the blank labels). Modify the bottom margin if necessary to ensure the footer will display on the page if printed. Save this as the end results file.

8 Submit file(s) as directed by your instructor.

CONTENT-BASED ASSESSMENTS

PROJECT FILES

For Project 1A Culinary Bistro Mailing Part 4, you will need the following files:

Lastname_Firstname_1A_Bistro_Addresses (from Part 3 of this project)
Lastname_Firstname_1A_Bistro_Letter (from Part 1 of this project)

You will save your documents as:

Lastname_Firstname_1A_Bistro_Form_Letters
Lastname_Firstname_1A_Bistro_Addresses

PROJECT RESULTS

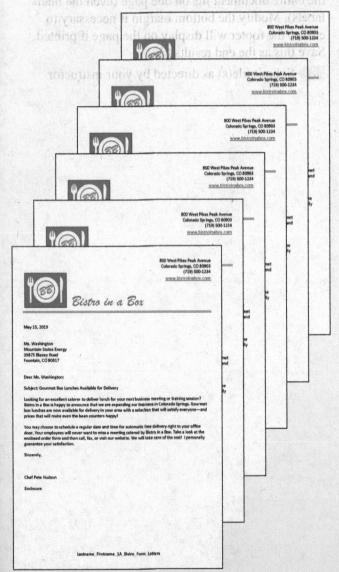

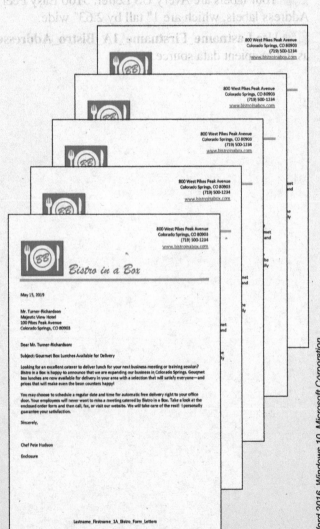

FIGURE 1.4 Project 1A, Part 4 Bistro Form Letters

(Project 1A Part 4 Culinary Bistro Form Letters continues on the next page)

Word 2016, Windows 10, Microsoft Corporation.

CONTENT-BASED ASSESSMENTS

| GO! Make It | **Project 1A Part 4 Culinary Bistro Form Letters** (continued) |

1 From your **Culinary Bistro Mailing** folder, locate and open **Lastname_Firstname_1A_Bistro_Addresses**. Add a column to the table for the recipients' titles, such as Mr. or Ms., and enter appropriate titles. Save and close the file.

2 From your **Culinary Bistro Mailing** folder, locate and open your file **Lastname_Firstname_1A_Bistro_Letter**. Save the file as **Lastname_Firstname_1A_Bistro_Main_Letter** so that you will not confuse it with your end results file. Use mail merge to create a new document containing 11 form letters that look like the letter shown in Figure 1.4.

3 In the footer of the main letter file, delete the field name code. In the footer, enter your *last name* and *first name* and **1A Bistro Form Letters**. This new footer will show on each of the form letters. Save the file.

4 The data source is **Lastname_Firstname_1A_Bistro_Addresses**. Sort by zip code from low to high. Insert a proper business letter address block and greeting line. Preview the document and compare with Figure 1.4.

5 Verify that the letters are properly formatted in the merge preview, and go back to fix as needed. Save **Lastname_Firstname_1A_Bistro_Main_Letter**.

6 At the end of the merge, choose to *Edit individual letters* to create a new file with the 11 letters, one on each page.

7 Save the end results file with the 11 letters in your **Culinary Bistro Mailing** folder as **Lastname_Firstname_1A_Bistro_Form_Letters**.

8 Submit file(s) as directed by your instructor.

> **END | You have completed Project 1A**

OUTCOMES-BASED ASSESSMENTS

Apply skills from these objectives:

1 Create a New Document from an Existing Document
2 Change Document and Paragraph Layout
3 Insert and Format Graphics
4 Use Special Character and Paragraph Formatting
5 Change and Reorganize Text
6 Use Proofing Options
7 Preview and Print a Document

GO! Think | Project 1B Culinary Gala Mailing: Part 1 Culinary Gala Letter

 PROJECT FILES

For Project 1B Culinary Gala Mailing Part 1, you will need the following files:

w1B_PPCC_Logo
w1B_Gala_Letter

You will save your document as:

Lastname_Firstname_1B_Gala_Letter

You are the president of the local chapter of the American Culinary Federation. You have been asked to send a letter to invite local businesses to attend a Chefs' Gala Celebration and fundraising event at a local hotel. The chefs participating are local chefs, and they will cook their favorite menu items to raise money for local charities.

1 Create a folder in which to save your files for this project called **Culinary Gala Mailing**.

2 From the student files that accompany this text, locate and open the file **w1B_Gala_Letter**, and then save the file in your **Culinary Gala Mailing** folder as **Lastname_Firstname_1B_Gala_Letter**.

3 Add the file name to the footer as a Quick Parts field.

4 Create a letterhead using the first three lines in the letter. Insert the **w1B_PPCC_Logo** graphic. Insert a paragraph border to separate the letterhead from the text in the letter.

5 Edit to compose a one-page proper business letter inviting local businesses to attend the gala.

6 Insert your own local charities as a list. Add the names of community organizations and charities in your area that the gala will support. These may include any nonprofit organizations, including local food banks, rescue missions, and the American Culinary Education Fund.

7 Change the line spacing, paragraph spacing, blank lines, and text in the letter as appropriate for a properly formatted one-page business letter. Reference the example of a properly formatted business letter in the previous project or see proper business letter requirements in Appendix A.

8 Preview the document and go back to adjust as needed. Adjust margins and font size appropriately to make the letter fit neatly on one page.

9 Check the letter for spelling and grammar errors, and correct any errors found.

10 Save the document, and submit the letter file as directed by your instructor.

OUTCOMES-BASED ASSESSMENTS

GO! Think Project 1B Part 2 Culinary Gala Flyer

Apply skills from these objectives:

1 Create a New Document from an Existing Document

2 Change Document and Paragraph Layout

3 Insert a SmartArt Graphic

4 Insert Footnote

5 Insert and Format Graphics

6 Use Special Character and Paragraph Formatting

7 Change and Reorganize Text

8 Create and Format a Table

9 Create and Modify Lists

10 Set and Modify Tab Stops

11 Use Proofing Options

12 Preview and Print a Document

13 Save a Document as a PDF

 PROJECT FILES

For Project 1B Culinary Gala Mailing Part 2, you will need the following files:

New blank Word document

w1B_PPCC_Logo

You will save your documents as:

Lastname_Firstname_1B_Gala_Flyer

Lastname_Firstname_1B_Gala_Flyer_PDF

You are the president of the local chapter of the American Culinary Federation. You are planning a Chefs' Gala celebration and fund-raising event at a local hotel. The chefs participating are local chefs, and they will cook their favorite menu items to raise money for local charities. In this project, you will create a one-page flyer that explains details about the Chefs' Gala and fund-raising event. The flyer will be used to encourage businesses to attend your event.

1 Open a new blank Word document, and then save the file in your **Culinary Gala Mailing** folder as **Lastname_Firstname_1B_Gala_Flyer**.

2 Add the file name to the footer as a Quick Parts field.

3 Add an appropriate title.

4 After the title, apply a two-column format, and use both columns to display the flyer information.

5 Use small caps, various font sizes, and colors throughout the document.

6 Refer to the letter in Part 1 of this project for cost, date, time, and reservation information as you compose the flyer.

7 Include the same local charities that will benefit from this event as were listed in the letter in Part 1 of this project. Format the list of charities in a table, and format the table using a design to match other parts of the flyer.

8 Do some research to come up with items for a tempting menu! Use real or made-up restaurants.

9 Apply paragraph borders and paragraph shading.

10 Create a text box with the ticket information, and then change the border and shading to match the other colors in the document.

11 Include a SmartArt Picture List to display chef photos and their restaurant names. Search Microsoft Office Clip Art or Office.com to find chef photos to insert in your SmartArt.

12 Use additional Microsoft clip art or other graphics, including the logo file **w1B_PPCC_Logo**.

13 Check for spelling and grammar errors, and correct any errors you find.

14 For best visual results, apply document design principles: Use formatting consistently rather than randomly. Apply contrast by making titles large and bold compared to body text. Apply design proximity by minimizing space after each title paragraph. Align all neatly.

15 Preview the document, and go back to adjust as needed. Save the document.

16 Save the document again as a PDF file with the name **Lastname_Firstname_1B_Gala_Flyer_PDF**.

17 Submit file(s) as directed by your instructor.

OUTCOMES-BASED ASSESSMENTS

Apply skills from these objectives:

1 Create Mailing Labels Using Mail Merge
2 Format a Table
3 Change Document and Paragraph Layout
4 Preview and Print a Document

GO! Think   Project 1B Part 3 Culinary Gala Mailing Labels

 PROJECT FILES

For Project 1B Culinary Gala Mailing Part 3, you will need the following files:

New blank Word document
w1B_Gala_Addresses

You will save your document as:

Lastname_Firstname_1B_Gala_Labels

1 From the student files that accompany this text, locate and copy the file **w1B_Gala_Addresses** to your **Culinary Gala Mailing** folder.

2 Starting with a new blank Word document, you will use mail merge to create mailing labels. So that you will not confuse it with your end results file, save the file as **Lastname_Firstname_1B_Gala_Labels_Main** in your **Culinary Gala Mailing** folder.

3 Your labels are Avery US Letter, 5160 Easy Peel Address labels, which are 1" tall by 2.63" wide.

4 Your data source is your Culinary Gala Mailing file **w1B_Gala_Addresses**.

5 Arrange your labels and change spacing to ensure that all lines fit in the label area. Save the main document file.

6 After the merge is completed, *Edit individual labels* to create a new file with all 11 labels. Save the file as **Lastname_Firstname_1B_Gala_Labels**.

7 To the footer add the file name as a Quick Parts field. If necessary, delete blank lines or row(s) at the bottom of the table so that the entire document fits on one page (even the blank labels). Modify the bottom margin, if necessary, to ensure the footer will display on the page if printed. Save this end results file.

8 Submit file(s) as directed by your instructor.

OUTCOMES-BASED ASSESSMENTS

GO! Think   Project 1B Part 4 Culinary Gala Form Letters

Apply skills from these objectives:

1 Create a New Document from an Existing Document

2 Merge a Data Source and a Main Document

3 Preview and Print a Document

 PROJECT FILES

For Project 1B Culinary Gala Mailing Part 4, you will need the following files:

Lastname_Firstname_1B_Gala_Letter (from Part 1 of this project)
w1B_Gala_Addresses

You will save your document as:

Lastname_Firstname_1B_Gala_Form_Letters

1 From your **Culinary Gala Mailing** folder, locate and open your file **Lastname_Firstname_1B_Gala_Letter**. Save the file as **Lastname_Firstname_1B_Gala_Main_Letter** so that you will not confuse it with your end results file. Use mail merge to create properly formatted business letters.

2 In the footer of the main letter file, replace the field name code, typing in your *last name* and *first name* and **1B Gala Form Letters**. This new footer will show on each of the form letters.

3 The data source is your Culinary Gala Mailing file **w1B_Gala_Addresses**. Preview the document, and go back to adjust as needed. Save the main document file.

4 After the merge is completed, *Edit individual letters* to create a new file with all 11 form letters with proper business letter format.

5 Save this end results file as **Lastname_Firstname_1B_Gala_Form_Letters**.

6 Submit file(s) as directed by your instructor.

END | You have completed Project 1B

GO! Make It | Project 1C Food Costing

PROJECT FILES

For Project 1C, you will need the following files:

e1C_Food_Costing

e1C_Bistro_Logo

You will save your workbook as:

Lastname_Firstname_1C_Food_Costing

PROJECT RESULTS

Bistro in a Box
Gourmet Sandwiches

Menu Item	Cost	Selling Price	Food Cost Percentage
Traditional Club	$4.55	$11.00	41.36%
Southwest Chicken	$3.05	$9.50	32.11%
Ham and Cheese Favorite	$3.90	$10.25	38.05%
Simply Chicken	$3.50	$9.50	36.84%
Tasty Turkey	$3.47	$9.50	36.53%
Rancher's BBQ Beef	$5.09	$12.50	40.72%
Italian Hoagie	$4.90	$10.25	47.80%
Tuna Salad	$3.84	$9.50	40.42%
Pork Tenderloin	$5.17	$12.50	41.36%
Philly Cheesesteak	$3.95	$9.50	41.58%
		Average Food Cost Percentage	39.68%
		Minimum Food Cost Percentage	32.11%
		Maximum Food Cost Percentage	47.80%

Lastname_Firstname_1C_Food_Costing   Sandwiches

Excel 2016, Windows 10, Microsoft Corporation.

FIGURE 1.5 Project 1C Food Costing

(Project 1C Food Costing continues on the next page)

Apply skills from these objectives:

1 Enter Data in a Worksheet

2 Format Cells with Merge & Center

3 Chart Data to Create a Column Chart

4 Check Spelling in a Worksheet

5 Construct Formulas for Mathematical Operations

6 Edit Values in a Worksheet

7 Format a Worksheet

8 Use the SUM, AVERAGE, MIN, and MAX Functions

9 Navigate a Workbook and Rename Worksheets

10 Edit and Format Multiple Worksheets at the Same Time

11 Create a Summary Sheet

CONTENT-BASED ASSESSMENTS

1 ▸ Create a folder in which to store your files for this project called **Food Costing**. From the student files that accompany this text, copy the file, **e1C_Bistro_Logo**, to this folder.

2 ▸ From the student files that accompany this text, locate and open the file **e1C_Food_Costing**, and then save the file in your **Food Costing** folder as **Lastname_Firstname_1C_Food_Costing**. You will modify the workbook to match the worksheets shown in Figures 1.5, 1.6, and 1.7.

3 ▸ Group Sheet1, Sheet2, and Sheet3, and modify the group of sheets as follows:

- Change the top margin to 2", and set the worksheet to center horizontally on the printed page to match Figure 1.5.
- In the footer, insert the code for the file name.
- In the header, insert the file **e1C_Bistro_Logo**.
- For the column heading and other labels, enter text; adjust column widths and row heights; and format the font, size, alignment, and wrapping to match the figure.
- Merge and center the **Bistro in a Box** title and **Gourmet Sandwiches** subtitle. Format the font, size, and color to match Figure 1.5. Delete blank rows as needed.
- Enter a formula to calculate the cost of the first sandwich as a percentage of selling price. Copy the formula to compute the same thing for all the sandwiches.
- Use the AVERAGE, MIN, and MAX functions to calculate to match Figure 1.5.
- Format the cells to match the figure.
- Apply borders to match the figure.
- Ungroup the worksheets when done.

4 ▸ Rename the worksheet tabs of the first four ungrouped sheets and apply tab colors.

	Sheet1	Sheet2	Sheet3	Sheet4
New tab name	Sandwiches	Wraps	Salads	Summary
Tab color	Blue	Red	Green	Yellow

5 ▸ Modify and format the Summary worksheet as follows:

- Insert the codes for the file name and sheet name in the footer, and set the worksheet to center horizontally on the printed page to match Figure 1.6.
- Copy the **Bistro in a Box** title from one of the previous worksheets, and add it to the top of this worksheet. Merge and center the **Menu Item Food Cost** title, and format to match Figure 1.6.
- In the row with the column heading labels, use the keyboard command <Alt> + Enter after the words *Average*, *Minimum*, and *Maximum* to insert a line break.
- Adjust text format, borders and shading, row heights, and column widths to match the figure.
- Enter formulas using cell references from the **Sandwiches**, **Wraps**, and **Salads** worksheets to display the average, minimum, and maximum food cost percentages for the three categories, as shown in Figure 1.6.
- Format to match Figure 1.6.
- Insert a Clustered Column chart to visually display the data. Apply a Chart Layout, change the titles, and size and position the chart as shown in Figure 1.6.

(Project 1C Food Costing continues on the next page)

CONTENT-BASED ASSESSMENTS

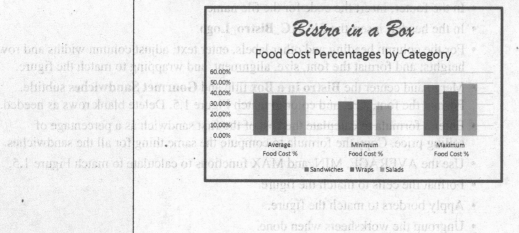

FIGURE 1.6 Project 1C Food Costing

5 On the Sandwiches worksheet, change the selling price of the Rancher's BBQ Beef and Pork Tenderloin to **$12.50** each. Note the changes to the figures on the Sandwiches worksheet and also the Summary worksheet.

7 Modify and format the Possibilities worksheet as follows:

- Insert the codes for the file name and sheet name in the footer, change the orientation to Landscape, and center horizontally on the page to match Figure 1.7.
- Merge and center the title and subtitle, and format to match Figure 1.7.
- Enter a formula to calculate a new selling price of the first sandwich based on the percentage increase in cell E3, using absolute cell referencing. Fill the formula for all the sandwiches. Also, calculate increased selling prices for each sandwich for 5% and 7% price increases.
- Calculate the new food cost percentages based on the current cost and the increased selling prices. Hint: Use the current selling price as the base. Fill and format as shown in Figure 1.7.

(Project 1C Food Costing continues on the next page)

GO! Make It **Project 1C Food Costing** (continued)

Possibilities -- Price Increase Based on Current Selling Price									
Gourmet Sandwiches									
Current Pricing				3%		5%		7%	
Menu Item	**Cost**	**Selling Price**	**Food Cost Percentage**	**Selling Price**	**Food Cost Percentage**	**Selling Price**	**Food Cost Percentage**	**Selling Price**	**Food Cost Percentage**
Traditional Club	$ 4.55	$ 11.00	41.36%	$ 11.33	40.16%	$ 11.55	39.39%	$ 11.77	38.66%
Southwest Chicken	3.05	9.50	32.11%	9.79	31.17%	9.98	30.58%	10.17	30.00%
Ham and Cheese Favorite	3.90	10.25	38.05%	10.56	36.94%	10.76	36.24%	10.97	35.56%
Simply Chicken	3.50	9.50	36.84%	9.79	35.77%	9.98	35.09%	10.17	34.43%
Tasty Turkey	3.47	9.50	36.53%	9.79	35.46%	9.98	34.79%	10.17	34.14%
Rancher's BBQ Beef	5.09	12.50	40.72%	12.88	39.53%	13.13	38.78%	13.38	38.06%
Italian Hoagie	4.90	10.25	47.80%	10.56	46.41%	10.76	45.53%	10.97	44.68%
Tuna Salad	3.84	9.50	40.42%	9.79	39.24%	9.98	38.50%	10.17	37.78%
Pork Tenderloin	5.17	12.50	41.36%	12.88	40.16%	13.13	39.39%	13.38	38.65%
Philly Cheesesteak	$ 3.95	$ 9.50	41.58%	9.79	40.37%	9.98	39.60%	10.17	38.86%
AVERAGE FOOD COST PERCENTAGE			39.68%		38.52%		37.79%		37.08%

Lastname_Firstname_1C_Food_Costing   Possibilities

Excel 2016, Windows 10, Microsoft Corporation.

FIGURE 1.7 Project 1C Food Costing

- Use the AVERAGE function to display the average food cost percentage for each price increase at the bottom of the worksheet.
- Format to match Figure 1.7. Adjust column widths and row heights if necessary so that all data is visible.

8 Check the worksheets for spelling and grammar errors, and correct any errors you find. Save the workbook and submit it as directed by your instructor.

END | You have completed Project 1C

OUTCOMES-BASED ASSESSMENTS

Project 1D Hudson Grill

Apply skills from these objectives:

1 Enter Data in a Worksheet
2 Construct and Copy Formulas and Use the SUM Function
3 Format Cells with Merge & Center and Cell Styles
4 Chart Data to Create a Chart
5 Check Spelling in a Worksheet
6 Construct Formulas for Mathematical Operations
7 Edit Values in a Worksheet
8 Format a Worksheet
9 Use the SUM, AVERAGE, MEDIAN, MIN, and MAX Functions
10 Navigate a Workbook and Rename Worksheets
11 Edit and Format Multiple Worksheets at the Same Time
12 Create a Summary Sheet

 PROJECT FILES

For Project 1D, you will need the following file:

e1D_Hudson_Grill

You will save your workbook as:

Lastname_Firstname_1D_Hudson_Grill

As manager of the Hudson Grill restaurant, you must analyze monthly sales data to determine totals for sales, cost of goods sold, and profit for each month and construct a summary for the quarter. It is also important to make a chart to depict this data.

1 Create a folder in which to store your files for this project called **Hudson Grill**.

2 Open the file **e1D_Hudson_Grill**, and then save it in your **Hudson Grill** folder as **Lastname_Firstname_1D_Hudson_Grill**.

3 Group Sheet1, Sheet2, and Sheet3, and modify the grouped sheets as follows:

- Change the orientation to Landscape.
- Set the worksheet to center horizontally and vertically on the printed page. Set gridlines to print.
- In the footer, insert the code for the file name.
- Set appropriate text wrapping, bold, column widths, row heights, and borders for the column heading titles.
- Enter a formula for each menu item to calculate total food cost, referencing the cells with the cost per item and plates purchased.
- Enter a formula to calculate total number of plates purchased.
- Enter a formula for each menu item to calculate percentage of total plates purchased.
- Enter a formula to calculate total cost of goods sold (total of the food costs).
- Enter a formula for each menu item to calculate the total sales referencing the cells with menu price and plates purchased.
- Enter a formula to calculate the total sales.
- Enter a formula to calculate the total profit on food by subtracting total cost of goods sold from total sales.
- Arrange and format title across the columns used. Format **The Hudson Grill** as the main title, and make the Monthly Sales row stand out.
- Format and align neatly. Apply appropriate cell styles, borders, and fill color.
- Make appropriate adjustments as needed so the grouped sheets clearly fit on one page each. Ungroup the worksheets when done.

4 Rename the worksheet tabs of the ungrouped sheets according to the month and year, and apply your choice of tab colors.

(Project 1D Hudson Grill continues on the next page)

OUTCOMES-BASED ASSESSMENTS

5 ▸ Rename the fourth sheet **1st Qtr Summary**.

- In the summary worksheet, use formulas to reference the cells from the monthly sales worksheets.
- Set the worksheet to center horizontally on the printed page.
- In the footer, insert the codes for the sheet and file names.
- Arrange and format neatly and professionally. Use borders, fills, cell styles, font sizes, and merge and center as appropriate.
- Insert a text box and arrow shape to point out that March had the highest profit.
- Create a chart that shows the first-quarter summary of sales and profit for each month. Move the chart to a separate sheet, and then name the sheet **1st Qtr Chart**. Apply appropriate style and layout. Add appropriate chart elements. Adjust the fonts to ensure readability.

6 ▸ Check the worksheets for spelling and grammar errors, and correct any errors you find. Save the workbook and submit it as directed by your instructor.

> **END | You have completed Project 1D**

CONTENT-BASED ASSESSMENTS

GO! Make It	Project 1E Recipe Database

Apply skills from these objectives:

1 Open and Save an Existing Database

2 Change the Structure of Tables and Add a Second Table

3 Create Table Relationships

4 Create a Query in Query Design

5 Sort Query Results

6 Specify Criteria in a Query

7 Specify Numeric Criteria in a Query

8 Use Compound Criteria in a Query

9 Create a Query Based on More Than One Table

10 Create Calculated Fields in a Query

11 Create a Form Using the Form Wizard

12 Create Reports Using the Report Wizard

13 Close a Database and Exit Access

PROJECT FILES

For Project 1E, you will need the following files:

a1E_Recipe_Database.accdb (Access file)

a1E_Recipe_Ingredients.xlsx (Excel file)

You will save your database as:

Lastname_Firstname_1E_Recipe_Database.accdb

PROJECT RESULTS

FIGURE 1.8 Project 1E Recipe Database—Recipe Ingredients Table.

(Project 1E Recipe Database continues on the next page)

1   Create a folder in which to store your files for this project called **Recipe Database**.

2   From the student files that accompany this text, locate the **a1E_Recipe_Ingredients** Excel workbook, and copy it into your **Recipe Database** folder.

3   From the student files that accompany this text, open **a1E_Recipe_Database**, and then save it to your **Recipe Database** folder as **Lastname_Firstname_1E_Recipe_Database**. Enable the content. Open the **1E Recipes** table, and make yourself familiar with the data in the table.

4   In the **1E Recipes** table, rename the Minutes Prep Time field to **Prep Time**. Apply *Best Fit* to all of the columns. Save and close the table.

5   Create a table as shown in Figure 1.8 by importing the **a1E_Recipe_Ingredients** Excel workbook.

- Use the first row as the column headings.
- Use **Ingredient ID** as the primary key.
- Name the table **Lastname_Firstname_1E_Recipe Ingredients**.
- Open the table, and become familiar with the information in the table. Apply *Best Fit* to all of the columns. Save and close the table.

6   Create a one-to-many relationship between the **1E Recipes** table and the **Lastname_Firstname_1E_Recipe_Ingredients** table using the **Recipe ID** field.

- Do not enforce referential integrity. Adjust the tables so that all fields are visible.
- Save and close the Relationships pane.

7   Open the **1E Recipes** table. Because you have created the relationship, you will see a plus sign or expand symbol to the left of each recipe name. Click the plus sign, and you will see the ingredients listed for each recipe. Close the table.

8   Create a form based on the **1E Recipes** table that can be used to enter more recipes. Use the Form Wizard accepting the default settings. Save the form with the name **Lastname_Firstname_1E_Recipes**, and then close the form.

9   Create a query using the **1E Recipes** table that answers the following question: *Which recipes are low-fat recipes?*

- Use the fields **Recipe Name**, **Menu Item**, **Source**, and **Low Fat**.
- Sort by **Menu Item** in ascending order in Design View.
- Run the query, and compare with Figure 1.9.
- Apply *Best Fit* to all of the columns. Save the query as **Lastname_Firstname_1E_Low_Fat**, and then close the query.

10   Create a compound query using the **1E Recipes** table that answers the following question: *Which individual appetizer or side dish menu items have less than 150 calories?*

- Use the fields **Recipe Name**, **Menu Item**, and **Calories**.
- Sort by **Menu Item** in ascending order in Design View.
- Run the query and compare with Figure 1.10.
- Apply Best Fit to all of the columns. Save the query as **Lastname_Firstname_1E_Low_Cal_App_and_Side**.

(Project 1E Recipe Database continues on the next page)

Lastname_Firstname_1E_Low_Fat			5/21/2019
Recipe Name	**Menu Item**	**Source**	**Low Fat**
Carol's Crab Cakes	Appetizer	Carol Lopez	☑
Stan's Spinach Onion Dip	Appetizer	Stan Wilson	☑
Faye's Frozen Delight	Dessert	Faye	☑
Nancy's Maple Salmon	Main dish	Nancy Martin	☑
Heavenly Pork Tenderloin	Main dish	Dad	☑
Artichoke Chicken	Main dish	Cousin Willie	☑
Extraordinary Green Beans	Side dish	Aunt Mary	☑
Favorite Fruit Salad	Side dish	Grandma	☑

Page 1

Access 2016, Windows 10, Microsoft Corporation.

FIGURE 1.9 Project 1E Recipe Database—Low-Fat Query

(Project 1E Recipe Database continues on the next page)

GO! Make It | Project 1E Recipe Database (continued)

Lastname_Firstname_1E_Total_Time 5/21/2019

Recipe Name	Prep Time	Cook or Chill Mi	Total Min	Total Hrs
Artichoke Chick	30	25	55.00	0.92
Ben's Bean Dip	15	60	75.00	1.25
Broccoli Casser	20	55	75.00	1.25
Carol's Crab Ca	30	10	40.00	0.67
Extraordinary G	15	10	25.00	0.42
Fabulous Flank	15	15	30.00	0.50
Favorite Fruit S	20	120	140.00	2.33
Faye's Frozen D	20	0	20.00	0.33
Heavenly Pork	15	15	30.00	0.50
Nancy's Maple	25	10	35.00	0.58
Paula's Pistachi	20	120	140.00	2.33
Peter's Peanut	15	240	255.00	4.25
Speedy Spuds	20	40	60.00	1.00
Stan's Spinach	20	45	65.00	1.08
Susan's Surpris	20	240	260.00	4.33
Victoria's Veggi	45	60	105.00	1.75

Page 1

FIGURE 1.10 Project 1E Recipe Database—Low-Cal App and Side Query

(Project 1E Recipe Database continues on the next page)

11 Create a calculated field query using the **1E Recipes** table that answers the question: *What is the total time it takes to prepare a recipe including the prep time and cook or chill minutes?*

- Use the fields **Recipe Name**, **Prep Time**, and **Cook or Chill Minutes**.

- Create a calculated field **Total Min** that calculates the **Prep Time** plus the **Cook or Chill Minutes**. Change the number format to *Standard*.

- Create another calculated field **Total Hrs** that divides the **Total Min** by **60**. Change the number format to *Standard*.

- Sort by **Recipe Name** in ascending order in Design View.

- Run the query, and compare with Figure 1.11.

- Apply *Best Fit* to all of the columns. Save the query as **Lastname_Firstname_1E_Total_Time**, and then close the query.

Lastname_Firstname_1E_Low_Cal_App_and_Side   8/14/2019

Recipe Name	Menu Item	Calories
Stan's Spinach Onion Dip	Appetizer	76
Ben's Bean Dip	Appetizer	114
Extraordinary Green Beans	Side dish	60
Favorite Fruit Salad	Side dish	118

Page 1

Access 2016, Windows 10, Microsoft Corporation.

FIGURE 1.11 Project 1E Recipe Database—Total Time Query

(Project 1E Recipe Database continues on the next page)

12 Create a query using the **1E Recipes** table that answers the question: *Which recipes serve four or more?*

- Use the **Recipe Name**, **Source**, **Menu Item**, and **Servings**.
- Sort by **Menu item** in ascending order in Design View.
- Run the query, and compare with Figure 1.12.
- Save the query as **Lastname_Firstname_1E_Serves 4+**, and then close the query.

Recipe Name	Source	Menu Item	Servings
Stan's Spinach Onion Dip	Stan Wilson	Appetizer	10
Carol's Crab Cakes	Carol Lopez	Appetizer	5
Victoria's Veggie Pizza	Cousin Vicky	Appetizer	4
Ben's Bean Dip	Uncle Ben	Appetizer	6
Susan's Surprise Pumpkin Pie	Susan Fisher	Dessert	10
Peter's Peanut Butter Pie	Peter Mayer	Dessert	8
Faye's Frozen Delight	Faye	Dessert	8
Paula's Pistachio Dessert	Paula Guiterrez	Dessert	9
Nancy's Maple Salmon	Nancy Martin	Main dish	4
Artichoke Chicken	Cousin Willie	Main dish	4
Fabulous Flank Steak	Frank Sui	Main dish	4
Heavenly Pork Tenderloin	Dad	Main dish	4
Extraordinary Green Beans	Aunt Mary	Side dish	6
Speedy Spuds	Mom	Side dish	10
Broccoli Casserole	Judy Jagger	Side dish	7
Favorite Fruit Salad	Grandma	Side dish	8

Lastname_Firstname_1E_Serves_4+   5/21/2019

Page 1

Access 2016, Windows 10, Microsoft Corporation.

FIGURE 1.12 Project 1E Recipe Database—Serves 4+ Query

(Project 1E Recipe Database continues on the next page)

13 Create a query using both tables that answers the following question: *What are the ingredients in Recipe 2, and how much of each ingredient is needed?*

- Use the **Recipe ID**, **Recipe Name**, **Ingredient**, and **Quantity** fields.

- Sort in ascending order by **Ingredient** in Design View.

- Run the query, and compare with Figure 1.13.

- Apply *Best Fit* to all of the columns. Save the query as **Lastname_Firstname_1E_Recipe_2_Ingred**, and then close the query.

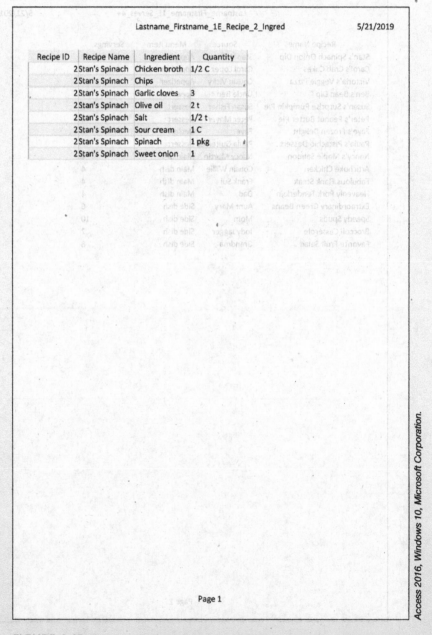

Lastname_Firstname_1E_Recipe_2_Ingred   5/21/2019

Recipe ID	Recipe Name	Ingredient	Quantity
2	Stan's Spinach	Chicken broth	1/2 C
2	Stan's Spinach	Chips	
2	Stan's Spinach	Garlic cloves	3
2	Stan's Spinach	Olive oil	2 t
2	Stan's Spinach	Salt	1/2 t
2	Stan's Spinach	Sour cream	1 C
2	Stan's Spinach	Spinach	1 pkg
2	Stan's Spinach	Sweet onion	1

Page 1

Access 2016, Windows 10, Microsoft Corporation.

FIGURE 1.13 Project 1E Recipe Database—Recipe 2 Ingredients Query

(Project 1E Recipe Database continues on the next page)

14 Use the Report Wizard to create a report matching Figure 1.14 using data from **1E Recipes** and **Lastname_Firstname_1E_Recipe_Ingredients**.

- Use the **Recipe Name, Ingredient, Quantity**, and **Comments** fields.
- View data by **Recipe Name**.
- Do not group or sort the data.
- Accept the *Stepped* Layout and *Portrait* Orientation default settings.
- Save the report as **Lastname_Firstname_1E_Recipe_Ingredients**. Close the report.

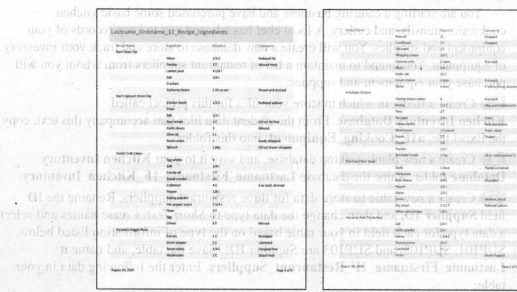
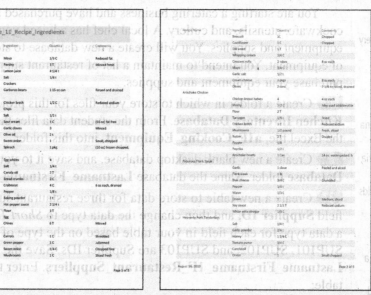

FIGURE 1.14 Project 1E Recipe Database—Recipe Ingredients Report

15 Close the database, and submit it as directed by your instructor.

END | You have completed Project 1E

OUTCOMES-BASED ASSESSMENTS

GO! Think   Project 1F Kitchen Inventory Database

Apply skills from these objectives:

1 Create a Table and Define Fields in a Blank Desktop Database

2 Change the Structure of Tables and Add a Second Table

3 Create and Use a Form to Add and Delete Records

4 Create Table Relationships

5 Create a Query in Query Design

6 Sort Query Results

7 Specify Criteria in a Query

8 Specify Numeric Criteria in a Query

9 Use Compound Criteria in a Query

10 Create Calculated Fields in a Query

11 Create Reports Using Report Wizard

12 Modify the Design of a Report

13 Close a Database and Exit Access

 PROJECT FILES

For Project 1F, you will need the following files:

New blank Access database
a1F_Cooking_Equipment (Excel file)

You will save your database as:

Lastname_Firstname_1F_Kitchen_Inventory

You are starting a catering business and have purchased some basic kitchen cookware, utensils, and cutlery. A local chef has advised you to keep records of your equipment and supplies. You will create a new database to store and track your inventory of equipment. You intend to maintain a list of restaurant suppliers from whom you will purchase your equipment and supplies.

1 Create a folder in which to store your files for this project called **Kitchen Inventory Database**. From the student data files that accompany this text, copy the Excel file, **a1F_Cooking_Equipment**, into this folder.

2 Create a new blank desktop database, and save it to your **Kitchen Inventory Database** folder. Name the database **Lastname_Firstname_1F_Kitchen_Inventory**.

3 Create a new table to store data for three restaurant suppliers. Rename the ID field **Supplier ID**, and then change the data type to *Short Text*. Create names and select a data type for each field in your table based on the type of information listed below. SUP101, SUP102, and SUP103 are Supplier IDs. Save the table, and name it **Lastname_Firstname_1F_Restaurant_Suppliers**. Enter the following data in your table:

SUP101	SUP102	SUP103
King of Culinary Supplies	Baker's Dream	Wholesale Kitchen Equipment
5432 North Nevada Avenue	90 Frontage Road	6789 Pinion Bluffs Parkway
Colorado Springs	Denver	Colorado Springs
CO	CO	CO
80903	80266	80920
719-555-3211	303-555-4567	719-555-4958
www.kingofculinary.com	www.bakersdream.com	www.kitchenequip.com

4 Create a form for your table, and save it with the default name.

5 Search the Internet to find at least one additional supplier that sells cooking supplies or equipment. Using the form, enter the additional supplier information into your table.

6 Create a new table by importing the Excel workbook **a1F_Cooking_Equipment** into your database. Allow Access to add the primary key field. Name the table **Lastname_Firstname_1F_Cooking_Equipment**.

(Project 1F Kitchen Inventory Database continues on the next page)

OUTCOMES-BASED ASSESSMENTS

7 Create a relationship between the two tables using a field that is common to both tables. Enforce referential integrity.

8 Create queries to answer the following questions, and include fields of your choice. Enter criteria and sort appropriately in Design View. Save and name each query using words that are descriptive of the query results.

- Select a city, and then display only the suppliers that are in that city. *What is the street address for each supplier in that city?*

- *What baking pans are in your existing inventory, and what is the description of each pan?*

- *For which items do you have more than eight in your inventory?*

- *Based on the quantity in stock and the unit price, what is the value of each item?*

- *What are the sizes and quantities on hand for the items in the cutlery and utensils categories?*

- *Which items are missing a price?* Hint: Use *Is Null* for the criteria.

9 Run the query that calculates item value. Add a *Total Row* to the bottom of the query results to compute the total value of your equipment.

10 Search the Internet to find prices for the missing items, and then enter the prices in the table.

11 Create a report that displays your cooking equipment inventory. Group and sort the records as you desire. Modify the column widths and change the orientation, as needed so that all data is visible. Name and save the report.

12 Close the database, and submit it as directed by your instructor.

END | You have completed Project 1F

CONTENT-BASED ASSESSMENTS

Apply skills from these objectives:

1 Edit a Presentation in Normal View
2 Add Pictures to a Presentation
3 Print and View a Presentation
4 Edit an Existing Presentation
5 Format Slides
6 Apply Slide Transitions
7 Format Numbered and Bulleted Lists
8 Insert Text Boxes and Shapes
9 Format Objects
10 Remove Picture Backgrounds and Insert WordArt
11 Create and Format a SmartArt Graphic
12 Create and Modify Tables

 PROJECT FILES

For Project 1G, you will need the following files:

p1G_Community_Garden
p1G_Club_Logo
p1G_Garden
p1G_Hands
p1G_Garden_Photo
p1G_Grass
p1G_PPCC_Logo
p1G_Tomato
p1G_Vegetables
p1G_Vegetables_2
p1G_Veggie_Tree

You will save your presentation as:

Lastname_Firstname_1G_Community_Garden

PROJECT RESULTS

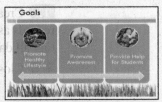
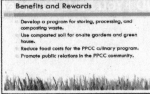

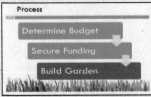

PowerPoint 2016, Windows 10, Microsoft Corporation.

FIGURE 1.15 Project 1G Community Garden Presentation

(Project 1G Community Garden Presentation continues on the next page)

1   Your culinary arts club has created a community garden. You have been asked to create a presentation about your project for students at another college.

2   Create a new folder to store your files for this project, and name the folder **Community Garden**.

3   From the student files that accompany this text, locate the Culinary, PowerPoint, Community Garden project files, and copy all the **p1G** files for this project into your **Community Garden** folder.

4   Open the file **p1G_Community_Garden** from your **Community Garden** folder, and save it as **Lastname_Firstname_1G_Community_Garden**.

5   Insert a header and footer for the notes and handouts.

- Display a date that updates automatically.
- Add to the footer the page number and **Presented by Firstname Lastname**.

6   On Slide 1 as shown in Figure 1.15:

- Create a WordArt title with the text **Community Garden**.
- Change the background style graphics to picture, and insert the **p1G_Grass** picture as the background.
- Insert the **p1G_PPCC_Logo** picture in the upper left corner.
- Insert the **p1G_Club_Logo** picture in the upper right corner.

7   Insert a new slide with the Title and Content layout, as shown in Figure 1.15.

- In the title placeholder, enter: **Purpose**.
- In the content placeholder, enter:

    Provide an educational opportunity for PPCC Culinary Arts students to cultivate green space and promote awareness of the environment, health, and nutrition among students, faculty, and staff.

- Insert the **p1G_Hands** picture in the upper right corner.
- Grass will be added to the slides in step 15.

8   Insert a new slide with Title and Content layout, as shown in Figure 1.15.

- In the title placeholder, type **Goals**.
- Insert a SmartArt List *Continuous Picture* with the following information:

Picture file to Insert	p1G_Vegetables	p1G_Tomato	p1G_Vegetables_2
Text to Enter	Promote Healthy Lifestyle	Promote Awareness	Provide Help for Students

- On the Notes pane, type the following note:

    A community garden will promote awareness of the impact WE have on our environment. It will also provide for the many needs of the students in the PPCC community.

(Project 1G Community Garden Presentation continues on the next page)

9 Insert a new slide with the Title and Content layout.

- In the title placeholder, type **Benefits and Rewards**.
- Use a bulleted list, and type the following information:

  Develop a program for storing, processing, and composting waste.

  Use composted soil for on-site gardens and greenhouse.

  Reduce food costs for the PPCC culinary program.

  Promote public relations in the PPCC community.

10 Reuse all four slides from the **p1G_Garden** presentation.

11 On the first new slide, Slide 5, format the text *Green* to match Figure 1.15.

12 On the second new slide, Slide 6, edit the SmartArt to match Figure 1.15.

13 In Slide 8, insert the **p1G_Veggie_Tree** picture to match Figure 1.15.

14 Insert a new slide with Title and Content layout to match Figure 1.15.

- Title it **Financial Contributors**.
- Insert a table with the following information:

Organization	Amount
PPCC Foundation	$1,500
Student Government	3,000
Culinary Arts Club	500
Community Business Donations	1,000
Total	$6,000

15 Select Slides 2 through 9. You will place the grass at the bottom of each slide, positioned a bit lower than on Slide 1, to match Figure 1.15.

- Change the background style for all of the selected slides to a picture by using the **p1G_Grass** picture.
- In the Format Background pane, set Offset top to 0% and Offset bottom to –40%.

16 After Slide 9, insert a new slide with Picture with Caption layout to match Figure 1.15.

- Insert the **p1G_Garden_Photo** picture.
- Format the background style to Solid Fill Standard Green color.
- Insert the **p1G_PPCC_Logo** picture in the upper left corner.
- Enter the title text **PPCC Community Garden Completed June 2016**.
- Under the title caption, enter **For further information, contact the Culinary Arts Department at Pikes Peak Community College.**

17 To all slides apply the Transition *Cover*.

18 Insert the slide number on each slide but do not include it on the title slide.

19 Run the slide show, and proofread.

20 Save the presentation, and submit it as directed by your instructor.

END | You have completed Project 1G

OUTCOMES-BASED ASSESSMENTS

GO! Think Project 1H Healthy Recipe Presentation

 PROJECT FILES

For Project 1H, you will need the following file:

New blank PowerPoint presentation

You will save your presentation as:

Lastname_Firstname_1H_Healthy_Recipe

Apply skills from these objectives:

1 Create a New Presentation
2 Edit a Presentation in Normal View
3 Add Pictures to a Presentation
4 Print and View a Presentation
5 Format Slides
6 Apply Slide Transitions
7 Format Numbered and Bulleted Lists
8 Insert Online Pictures
9 Format Objects
10 Create and Format a SmartArt Graphic
11 Customize Slide Backgrounds and Themes
12 Animate a Slide Show
13 Create and Modify Tables
14 Create and Modify Charts

1 Your culinary arts club is participating in a neighborhood health fair, and you have been asked to create a presentation telling how to prepare a healthy recipe.

2 Select a published recipe, an old family recipe, or one of your own creations. Keep in mind that you must cite your source(s) in your presentation.

3 Create a new folder for this project, and name it **Healthy Recipe**.

4 Create a new blank PowerPoint presentation file. Save the file in your **Healthy Recipe** folder as **Lastname_Firstname_1H_Healthy_Recipe**.

5 Include a list of ingredients, preparation directions, a photo of the finished recipe, and nutritional information such as calories, fat, fiber, and carbohydrates.

6 In the Notes and Handouts footer, enter your name and **1H_Healthy_Recipe**.

7 Insert the following footer on the slides: **Presented by Firstname Lastname**.

8 Apply a design theme of your choice.

9 Use at least three different slide layouts. Follow the 6 × 6 rule. (No more than six lines of text and no more than six words in a line.)

10 Use WordArt on at least one slide.

11 Insert online pictures or photos related to your topic.

12 Use SmartArt.

13 Create a table or chart to display information about your recipe.

14 Apply transitions to all slides, and if you like, add simple animation.

15 In the Notes pane, enter notes about the points you plan to make during the presentation.

16 Run the slide show, and proofread.

17 Save the presentation, and submit it as directed by your instructor.

END | You have completed Project 1H

Discipline Specific Projects

You will complete the following discipline specific projects:

Word	GO! Make It | Project 2A Healthcare Dental Mailing (p. 36)
	Part 1 Create a proper business letter to match visual summary. Use graphics, no spacing style, and character and paragraph formatting.
	Part 2 Create a newsletter to match visual summary. Use graphics, character and paragraph formatting, table, tab stops, footnotes, and save as PDF.
	Part 3 Create mailing labels to match visual summary. Edit table, use character and paragraph formatting, and mail merge.
	Part 4 Create form letters to match visual summary. Edit table and use mail merge.
	GO! Think | Project 2B Healthcare Medical Mailing (p. 44)
	Part 1 Create a business letter to inform staff about a new medical facility. Use graphics, no spacing style, and character and paragraph formatting.
	Part 2 Create an MLA paper about diet and exercise. Use paragraph formatting, page numbering, footnotes, citations, Source Manager, and save as PDF.
	Part 3 Create mailing labels. Edit table, use character and paragraph formatting, and mail merge.
	Part 4 Create form letters. Use mail merge.
Excel	GO! Make It | Project 2C Medical Invoice (p. 49)
	Create a medical invoice workbook to match visual summary. Enter data, formulas, and functions; chart data; group worksheets; format; and make summary sheet.
	GO! Think | Project 2D Medical Supplies Order (p. 53)
	Create a workbook to keep track of medical supplies and orders. Enter data, formulas, and functions; chart data; group worksheets; format; and make summary sheet.
Access	GO! Make It | Project 2E Inventory Database (p. 55)
	Work with an inventory database to match visual summary. Add tables, edit table structure, and join tables; create forms and reports; and create queries with compound criteria, calculated fields, and grouping.
	GO! Think | Project 2F Billing Database (p. 65)
	Work with a database to keep track of suppliers and inventory. Add a table, edit table structure, and join tables; create forms and reports; and create queries with compound criteria, calculated fields, and grouping.
PowerPoint	GO! Make It | Project 2G Lowering Blood Pressure Presentation (p. 67)
	Create a blood pressure presentation to match visual summary. Format slides and work with pictures, tables, charts, WordArt, SmartArt, animation, transitions, backgrounds, and themes.
	GO! Think | Project 2H Patient Presentation (p. 70)
	Create a presentation for patients living with a particular disease or condition. Format slides, and work with pictures, tables, charts, WordArt, SmartArt, animation, transitions, backgrounds, and themes.

Apply skills from these objectives:

1 Create a New Document from an Existing Document

2 Change Document and Paragraph Layout

3 Insert and Format Graphics

4 Use Special Character and Paragraph Formatting

5 Change and Reorganize Text

6 Use Proofing Options

7 Preview and Print a Document

GO! Make It — Project 2A Healthcare Dental Mailing: Part 1 Healthcare Dental Letter

📁 PROJECT FILES

For Project 2A Healthcare Dental Mailing Part 1, you will need the following files:

w2A_Dental_Letter

w2A_Dental_Logo

You will save your document as:

Lastname_Firstname_2A_Dental_Letter

PROJECT RESULTS

Colorado Dynamic Dentistry

2000 W. Broadmoor Bluffs Parkway, Ste. 208, Colorado Springs, CO 80904
719-555-8899 www.dynamicdent.com

May 15, 2019

Mr. Carl Martinez
700 Aspen Drive
Colorado Springs, CO 80911

Dear Mr. Martinez:

Subject: New Office and Expanded Dental Care!

Colorado Dynamic Dentistry will be opening our new office at 2000 W. Broadmoor Bluffs Parkway on Monday, September 10.

Our new office has allowed us to expand our services and provide additional services. In addition to Dr. Mac Olson, D.D.S. and Dr. William Martinez, D.D.S., we hired Dr. Karla Reed, D.D.S., who has extensive experience in cosmetic dentistry, and Dr. Kenneth Walgreen, D.D. S., who specializes in Pediatric Dentistry. You can go to our website at www.dynamicdent.com to see a virtual tour of our new office.

Each member of our dental staff is fully committed to providing affordable, professional dental service for you and your family. Offering both general and cosmetic dental services, we work within all phases of dental care, including root canal therapy, porcelain crowns and bridges, and teeth whitening. We offer preventive care, children's dentistry, and specialty care services.

Good dental habits can positively effect overall health, and our dentists and professional staff value their role in helping patients maintain and/or improve our patients' total wellness.

We accept most insurance plans and also refer those without insurance to our preferred patient program. If you need to make an appointment, please call our office at 719-555-8899.

The office is open six days per week, Monday through Thursday from 8:30 a.m. to 6 p.m. and 8:30 a.m. to 3 p.m. on Friday and Saturday. The office offers same-day appointments.

Let our dental professionals provide quality dental care for you and your family. We look forward to working with you.

Sincerely,

Dr. Mac Olson, D.D.S.

Lastname_Firstname_2A_Dental_Letter

Word 2016, Windows 10, Microsoft Corporation.

FIGURE 2.1 Project 2A, Part 1 Dental Letter

(Project 2A Part 1 Healthcare Dental Letter continues on the next page)

CONTENT-BASED ASSESSMENTS

1 Create a folder in which to save your files for this project called **Healthcare Dental Mailing**.

2 From the student files that accompany this text, locate and open the file **w2A_Dental_Letter**, and then save the file in the **Healthcare Dental Mailing** folder as **Lastname_Firstname_2A_Dental_Letter**. Use this file to create a properly formatted business letter. Make the following modifications so that the document looks like the one shown in Figure 2.1.

3 Insert a footer with the file name as a Quick Parts field in the footer.

4 Change the top margin to .5". Set the side and bottom margins to 1".

5 For the entire document, change the line spacing to single and change the paragraph spacing after to zero, and set all indents to zero.

6 In the letterhead, from your student files, insert the picture **w2A_Dental_Logo**. Size and position the logo in the letterhead.

7 At the top of the page, edit and align the text and format the fonts to match the letterhead at the top of the letter shown in Figure 2.1.

8 Add a top border to the blank line below the letterhead.

9 Make corrections and additions to the text, including size, capitalization, punctuation, and content to match the proper business letter format shown in Figure 2.1. Use the current date.

10 Format the letter by adding and removing blank lines to use proper vertical spacing, as shown in Figure 2.1.

11 Correct any spelling and grammar errors. Preview the document, and compare with Figure 2.1, making adjustments as needed.

12 Save the document, and submit it as directed by your instructor.

Apply skills from these objectives:

1 Create a New Document from an Existing Document

2 Change Document and Paragraph Layout

3 Insert a SmartArt Graphic

4 Insert a Footnote

5 Insert and Format Graphics

6 Use Special Character and Paragraph Formatting

7 Change and Reorganize Text

8 Create and Format a Table

9 Set and Modify Tab Stops

10 Use Proofing Options

11 Preview and Print a Document

12 Save a Document as a PDF

PROJECT FILES

For Project 2A Healthcare Dental Mailing Part 2, you will need the following files:

w2A_Dental_Newsletter
w2A_Dental_Logo
w2A_Basketball
w2A_Dentist

You will save your documents as:

Lastname_Firstname_2A_Dental_Newsletter
Lastname_Firstname_2A_Dental_Newsletter_PDF

PROJECT RESULTS

FIGURE 2.2 Project 2A, Part 2 Dental Newsletter

(Project 2A Part 2 Healthcare Dental Newsletter continues on the next page)

CONTENT-BASED ASSESSMENTS

1 From the student files that accompany this text, locate and copy the files **w2A_Dental_Logo, w2A_Basketball** and **w2A_Dentist** into the **Healthcare Dental Mailing** folder.

2 From the student files that accompany this text, locate and open the file **w2A_Dental_Newsletter**, and then save the file in the **Healthcare Dental Mailing** folder as **Lastname_Firstname_2A_Dental_Newsletter**. You will use this file to create a one-page newsletter. Make the following modifications so that the document looks like the one shown in Figure 2.2.

3 Edit the footer to match Figure 2.2. Add the text **Printed on Recycled Paper**, and insert the file name as a Quick Parts field.

4 Set margins and columns to match Figure 2.2.

5 Insert the **w2A_Dental_Logo** picture file. Set text wrapping, and then size and position it.

6 Enter and edit text as needed, and set tabs to match Figure 2.2.

7 Insert borders to match Figure 2.2.

8 Insert picture files, SmartArt, and a table. Position and format them to match Figure 2.2.

9 At the end of the first paragraph about mouth protectors, insert a footnote. Enter the footnote text: **ADA/National High School Athletics Partnership**.

10 Set line and paragraph spacing, align text, and format fonts to match Figure 2.2.

11 Check the newsletter for spelling and grammar errors, and correct any errors you find. Ensure that the newsletter fits on one page. Preview the document, and compare with Figure 2.2, making adjustments as needed.

12 Save the document in your **Healthcare Dental Mailing** folder.

13 Save the document again as a PDF file with the name **Lastname_Firstname_2A_Dental_Newsletter_PDF** in your **Healthcare Dental Mailing** folder.

14 Submit file(s) as directed by your instructor.

Project 2A Part 3 Healthcare Dental Mailing Labels

Apply skills from these objectives:

1 Create Mailing Labels Using Mail Merge
2 Format a Table
3 Change Document and Paragraph Layout
4 Preview and Print a Document

 PROJECT FILES

For Project 2A Healthcare Dental Mailing Part 3, you will need the following files:

New blank Word document
w2A_Dental_Addresses

You will save your documents as:

Lastname_Firstname_2A_Dental_Addresses
Lastname_Firstname_2A_Dental_Labels

PROJECT RESULTS

Firstname Lastname	Karla McWilliams	Jenny Jager
5555 College Way	1235 Woodmen Road	1050 Garden of the Gods Road
College Town, CO 80903	Colorado Springs, CO 80918	Colorado Springs, CO 80907
Nancy Martin	Rob Cunningham	Melissa Walker
16680 Roller Coaster Road	458 East Pikes Peak Avenue	7020 Tall Oak Drive
Colorado Springs, CO 80921	Colorado Springs, CO 80903	Colorado Springs, CO 80919
Ann Wallace	Larry Anderson	Janice Larson
3300 Mesa Road	2705 E. Platte Avenue	7900 North Academy Blvd.
Colorado Springs, CO 80904	Colorado Springs, CO 80909	Colorado Springs, CO 80920
Bev Hanes	Robert Valdez	Carl Martinez
700 Manitou Avenue	1700 Lake Woodmoor Drive	700 Aspen Drive
Manitou Springs, CO 80829	Monument, CO 80132	Colorado Springs, CO 80911

Lastname_Firstname_2A_Dental_Labels

Word 2016, Windows 10, Microsoft Corporation.

FIGURE 2.3 Project 2A, Part 3 Dental Mailing Labels

(Project 2A Part 3 Healthcare Dental Mailing Labels continues on the next page)

CONTENT-BASED ASSESSMENTS

1 From the student files that accompany this text, locate and open the file **w2A_Dental_Addresses**, and add yourself to the top of the mailing list. Save the file as **Lastname_Firstname_2A_Dental_Addresses** in the **Healthcare Dental Mailing** folder, and then close the file.

2 Starting with a new blank Word document, use mail merge to create a document that looks like the one shown in Figure 2.3. Your labels are Avery US Letter, 5160 Easy Peel Address labels, which are 1" tall by 2.63" wide.

3 The recipient data source is **Lastname_Firstname_2A_Dental_Addresses**.

4 When inserting the address block, notice that in this data source the first and last names are both in one Name column. Use Match Fields to match the Name column to First Name and do *not* match Last Name in the address block.

5 Ensure that all lines fit in the label area. To avoid confusing this file with the end results file, save this file in your **Healthcare Dental Mailing** folder as **Lastname_Firstname_Dental_Labels_Main**.

6 Preview the document, and compare with Figure 2.3, making adjustments as needed. Save the main document.

7 At the end of the Merge, *Edit individual labels* to create a new file with only the label text. Save your new address labels document in your **Healthcare Dental Mailing** folder as **Lastname_Firstname_2A_Dental_Labels**.

8 To the footer, add the file name as a Quick Parts field. Preview the document, and if necessary delete blank lines or row(s) at the bottom of the table so that the entire document fits on one page (even the blank labels). Modify the bottom margin if necessary to ensure the footer will display on the page if printed. Save this as the end results file.

9 Submit file(s) as directed by your instructor.

CONTENT-BASED ASSESSMENTS

Apply skills from these objectives:

1 Create a New Document from an Existing Document

2 Format a Table

3 Merge a Data Source and a Main Document

4 Preview and Print a Document

PROJECT FILES

For Project 2A Healthcare Dental Mailing Part 4, you will need the following files:

Lastname_Firstname_2A_Dental_Addresses (from Part 3 of this project)
Lastname_Firstname_2A_Dental_Letter (from Part 1 of this project)

You will save your documents as:

Lastname_Firstname_2A_Dental_Form_Letters
Lastname_Firstname_2A_Dental_Letter_Addresses

PROJECT RESULTS

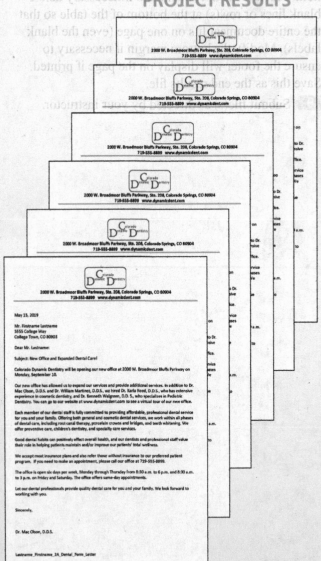
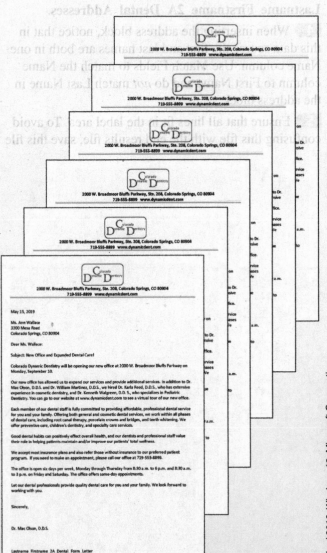

FIGURE 2.4 Project 2A, Part 4 Dental Form Letters

Word 2016, Windows 10, Microsoft Corporation.

(Project 2A Part 4 Healthcare Dental Form Letters continues on the next page)

CONTENT-BASED ASSESSMENTS

1 From your **Healthcare Dental Mailing** folder, locate and open your file **Lastname_Firstname_2A_Dental_Addresses**. Add two columns to the table. Edit and rearrange the content in the table to include separate first and last name columns and a column for recipient titles such as Mr. or Ms., and enter appropriate titles. Save and close the file.

2 You will use mail merge to create a new document containing 12 form letters that look like the one shown in Figure 2.4. From your **Healthcare Dental Mailing** folder, locate and open your file **Lastname_Firstname_2A_Dental_Letter**. Save the file as **Lastname_Firstname_2A_Dental_Main_Letter** to prevent confusion with your end results file.

3 In the footer of the main letter file, replace the field name code, typing in your *last name* and *first name* and **2A Dental Form Letters**. This new footer will show on each of the form letters. Save the main document file.

4 The data source is **Lastname_Firstname_2A_Dental_Letter_Addresses**. Insert a proper business letter address block and greeting line.

5 Preview the document, and compare with Figure 2.4. Verify that the letters are properly formatted in the merge preview, and go back to fix as needed. Save the main document.

6 At the end of the merge, choose to *Edit individual letters* to create a new file with the 12 letters, one on each page. Save the file with the 12 letters as **Lastname_Firstname_2A_Dental_Form_Letters** in your **Healthcare Dental Mailing** folder. Save this end results file.

7 Submit file(s) as directed by your instructor.

END | You have completed Project 2A

OUTCOMES-BASED ASSESSMENTS

Apply skills from these objectives:

1 Create a New Document from an Existing Document
2 Change Document and Paragraph Layout
3 Insert and Format Graphics
4 Use Special Character and Paragraph Formatting
5 Change and Reorganize Text
6 Use Proofing Options
7 Preview and Print a Document

 PROJECT FILES

For Project 2B Healthcare Medical Mailing Part 1, you will need the following files:

w2B_Global_Hospital_Logo
w2B_Medical_Letter

You will save your document as:

Lastname_Firstname_2B_Medical_Letter

You are the assistant to the vice president of facility development for a major hospital system. You want to send a letter to a doctor telling about a new medical facility your hospital system is planning to open.

1 Create a folder in which to save your files for this project called **Healthcare Medical Mailing**.

2 From the student files that accompany this text, locate and open the file **w2B_Medical_Letter**, and then save the file in your **Healthcare Medical Mailing** folder as **Lastname_Firstname_2B_Medical_Letter**.

3 Add the file name to the footer as a Quick Parts field.

4 Edit and properly format a one-page letter informing doctors about the new medical facility. Reference the example of a properly formatted business letter in the previous project or see proper business letter requirements in Appendix A.

5 Create a letterhead using the first three lines in the letter. Insert the **w2B_Global_Hospital_Logo** graphic. Insert a paragraph border to separate the letterhead from the text in the letter.

6 Research special hospital services or new medical technologies. Insert three or four special hospital services or new medical technologies as a list or table. Include one related to wellness or preventive health because with this letter you will be enclosing a paper about diet and exercise.

7 Set the line spacing, paragraph spacing, blank lines, and text as appropriate for a properly formatted one-page business letter.

8 Add a small paragraph or sentence indicating that you are enclosing, for the doctor's review, a paper about the health effects of diet and exercise.

9 Preview the document, and go back to adjust as needed. Compare with the example of a properly formatted business letter in the previous project or see proper business letter requirements in Appendix A. Adjust margins and font size appropriately to make the letter fit neatly on one page.

10 Check the letter for spelling and grammar errors, and correct any errors you find.

11 Save the document, and submit the letter file as directed by your instructor.

OUTCOMES-BASED ASSESSMENTS

GO! Think   Project 2B Part 2 Healthcare MLA Paper

 PROJECT FILES

For Project 2B Healthcare Medical Mailing Part 2, you will need the following file:
w2B_Diet_and_Exercise

You will save your documents as:
Lastname_Firstname_2B_Diet_and_Exercise
Lastname_Firstname_2B_ Diet_and_Exercise_PDF

You are a student in Dr. Hilary Kim's Physiology course. You have been asked to prepare a research paper about a topic related to wellness. You have researched the effects of diet and exercise. Dr. Kim is working with Global Hospital Corp. to develop their new Wellness Center in south Colorado Springs. She will be distributing the best wellness paper from her class to doctors in the Global Hospital Corp. system in the south Colorado Springs area.

1 From the student files that accompany this text, locate and open the file **w2B_Diet_and_Exercise**, and then save the file in your **Healthcare Medical Mailing** folder as **Lastname_Firstname_2B_Diet_and_Exercise**.

2 Add the file name to the footer as a Quick Parts field.

3 Using MLA Edition 8 research paper format, set line and paragraph spacing and enter the first page information. See Appendix B.

4 Format the page numbering and paragraph indents using MLA Edition 8 research paper format.

5 Insert two footnotes as follows:

- At the end of the second paragraph, enter a footnote: **The objective of the study was to examine the effects of exercise on total and intra-abdominal body fat overall and by level of exercise.**

- On the second page, enter a footnote at the end of the paragraph that begins *Exercise also has* and ends with the quote "*. . . intra-abdominal body fat," says Irwin.* Enter the text of the note: **Physical activity may provide a low-risk method of preventing weight gain. Unlike diet-induced weight loss, exercise-induced weight loss increases cardiorespiratory fitness levels.**

6 Using the MLA Edition 8 research paper format, enter three sources using the Source Manager as follows:

- The first source, **NIH News,** is a webpage with no named author, so use **U.S. Department of Health and Human Services** as the corporate author. Enter the title of the webpage: **NIH News.** Enter the date of publication, **2012 October 15**. For the date accessed, use the current date. For medium, enter **Web**.

- The second source is a book titled **Cardiovascular Physiology, Seventh Edition**. The authors are **Mohrman, David and Lois Heller.** It was published in **2010** in **New York** by **McGraw-Hill Professional**. For medium, enter **Print**.

(Project 2B Part 2 Healthcare MLA Paper continues on the next page)

- The third source is a book titled **Exercise for Mood and Anxiety: Proven Strategies for Overcoming Depression and Enhancing Well-Being**. The authors are **Otto, Michael and Jasper A. J. Smits**. It was published in **2011** in **New York** by **Oxford University Press, USA**. For medium, enter **Print**.

7 Using the MLA Edition 8 research paper format, insert three citations as follows:

- At the end of the first paragraph, enter a citation for **Otto**. Edit to include page **3** in the citation.

- On the second page, in the paragraph that begins *Other positive effects*, at the end of the second sentence right after *blood flow increases substantially*, enter a citation for **Mohrman**. Edit to include page **195** in the citation.

- At the bottom of the second page, at the end of the paragraph beginning *A recent study* and ending with *can sustain weight loss*, enter a citation for **U.S. Department of Health and Human Services**.

8 Create a reference page using the MLA Edition 8 research paper format.

9 Preview, proof, and correct as needed. Save the document.

10 Save the document again as a PDF.

11 Submit file(s) as directed by your instructor.

(Project 2B Part 2 Healthcare MLA Paper continues on the next page)

OUTCOMES-BASED ASSESSMENTS

Apply skills from these objectives:

1 Create Mailing Labels Using Mail Merge
2 Format a Table
3 Change Document and Paragraph Layout
4 Preview and Print a Document

GO! Think Project 2B Part 3 Healthcare Medical Mailing Labels

 PROJECT FILES

For Project 2B Healthcare Medical Mailing Part 3, you will need the following files:

New blank Word document
w2B_Medical_Addresses

You will save your document as:

Lastname_Firstname_2B_Medical_Labels

1 From the student files that accompany this text, locate and copy the file **w2B_Medical_Addresses** to your **Healthcare Medical Mailing** folder.

2 Start with a new blank Word document. To prevent confusion with the end results file, save the file as **Lastname_Firstname_2B_Medical_Labels_Main** in your **Healthcare Medical Mailing** folder.

3 Use mail merge to create labels. Your labels are Avery US Letter, 5160 Easy Peel Address labels, which are 1" tall by 2.63" wide.

4 Use **w2B_Medical_Addresses** as your data source. Use Match Fields to insert proper and complete names and addresses.

5 Arrange your labels and change spacing to ensure that all lines fit in the label area. Save the main document file.

6 After the merge is completed, *Edit individual labels* to create a new file with all the labels. Save the document as **Lastname_Firstname_2B_Medical_Labels**.

7 To the footer, add the file name as a Quick Parts field. If necessary, delete blank lines or row(s) at the bottom of the table so that the entire document fits on one page (even the blank labels). Modify the bottom margin, if necessary, to ensure the footer will display on the page if printed. Save this end results file.

8 Submit file(s) as directed by your instructor.

OUTCOMES-BASED ASSESSMENTS

GO! Think   Project 2B Part 4 Healthcare Medical Form Letters

 PROJECT FILES

For Project 2B Healthcare Medical Mailing Part 4, you will need the following files:

Lastname_FirstName_2B_Medical_Letter (from Part 1 of this project)
w2B_Medical_Addresses

You will save your document as:

Lastname_Firstname_2B_Medical_Form_Letters

1 From your **Healthcare Medical Mailing** folder, locate and open your file **Lastname_Firstname_2B_Medical_Letter**. Save the file as **Lastname_Firstname_2B_Medical_Main_Letter** to prevent confusion with your end results file. Use mail merge to create properly formatted business letters.

2 In the footer of the main letter file, replace the field name code, typing in your *last name* and *first name* and **2B Medical Form Letters**. This new footer will show on each of the form letters.

3 Use mail merge and filter the data source, the student data file **w2B_Medical_Addresses**, to create properly formatted business letters for only the doctors in Colorado Springs. Use Match Fields to insert proper and complete names and addresses. Save the main document file.

4 After the merge is completed, *Edit individual letters* to create a new file with all 18 form letters with proper business letter format.

5 Save this end results file as **Lastname_Firstname_2B_Medical_Form_Letters**.

6 Submit file(s) as directed by your instructor.

END | You have completed Project 2B

CONTENT-BASED ASSESSMENTS

GO! Make It   Project 2C Medical Invoice

Apply skills from these objectives:

1 Enter Data in a Worksheet

2 Construct and Copy Formulas and Use the SUM Function

3 Format Cells with Merge & Center and Cell Styles

4 Chart Data to Create a Column Chart

5 Check Spelling in a Worksheet

6 Construct Formulas for Mathematical Operations

7 Edit Values in a Worksheet

8 Format a Worksheet

9 Use the SUM, AVERAGE, MEDIAN, MIN, and MAX Functions

10 Navigate a Workbook and Rename Worksheets

11 Edit and Format Multiple Worksheets at the Same Time

12 Create a Summary Sheet

 PROJECT FILES

For Project 2C, you will need the following file:

e2C_Invoice
e2C_ALLMED_Logo

You will save your workbook as:

Lastname_Firstname_2C_Invoice

PROJECT RESULTS

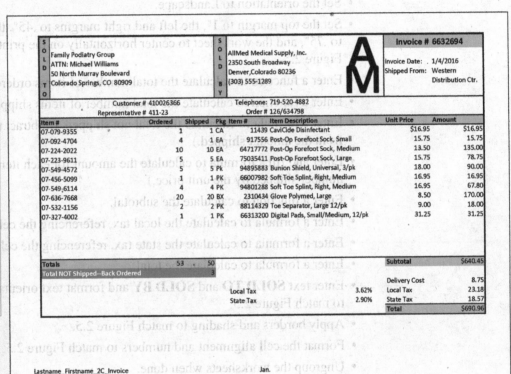

FIGURE 2.5 Project 2C Invoice

(Project 2C Medical Invoice continues on the next page)

1 Create a folder in which to store your files for this project called **Healthcare Invoice.**

2 From the student files that accompany this text, locate and open the file **e2C_Invoice**, and save the file in your **Healthcare Invoice** folder as **Lastname_Firstname_2C_Invoice.** You will modify the workbook to match the worksheets shown in Figures 2.5, 2.6, and 2.7.

3 Group Sheet1, Sheet2, Sheet3, and Sheet4 to simultaneously edit the group of sheets as follows:

- In the footer, insert the codes for the file name and the sheet name.
- Set the orientation to Landscape.
- Set the top margin to 1", the left and right margins to .45", the bottom margin to .75", and the worksheet to center horizontally on the printed page to match Figure 2.5.
- Enter a function to calculate the total number of items ordered.
- Enter a function to calculate the total number of items shipped.
- Enter a formula to calculate the total not shipped. (Subtract the amount ordered from the amount shipped.)
- Enter and fill a formula to calculate the amount for each item. (Multiply the number shipped by the unit price.)
- Enter a function to calculate the subtotal.
- Enter a formula to calculate the local tax, referencing the cell with the rate.
- Enter a formula to calculate the state tax, referencing the cell with the rate.
- Enter a formula to calculate the total.
- Enter text **SOLD TO** and **SOLD BY** and format text orientation and cell merging to match Figure 2.5.
- Apply borders and shading to match Figure 2.5.
- Format the cell alignment and numbers to match Figure 2.5.
- Ungroup the worksheets when done.
- Insert **e2C_ALLMED_Logo** on each sheet to match Figure 2.5.

4 Rename the worksheet tabs for each sheet.

- Rename Sheet1 **Jan**.
- Rename Sheet2 **Feb**.
- Rename Sheet3 **Mar**.
- Rename Sheet4 **Apr**.
- Rename Sheet5 **Summary**.

(Project 2C Medical Invoice continues on the next page)

Colorado Medical Supply, Inc.		
Invoice Summary for Family Podiatry Group		
January - April		
Month	**Items Shipped**	**Total Amount**
January	50	$690.96
February	49	2613.11
March	35	613.14
April	25	734.15

Lastname_Firstname_2C_Invoice   Summary

Excel 2016, Windows 10, Microsoft Corporation.

FIGURE 2.6 Project 2C Invoice

5 ▶ Complete the Summary sheet to match Figure 2.6.

- In the footer, insert the code for the file name and the code for the sheet name.
- Set the worksheet to center horizontally on the printed page.
- Enter formulas, referencing the cells with the number of items shipped for each month.
- Enter formulas, referencing the cells with the invoice total amounts for each month.
- Apply borders and shading, merge and center, bold, size columns, and format the cells to match Figure 2.6.

(Project 2C Medical Invoice continues on the next page)

CONTENT-BASED ASSESSMENTS

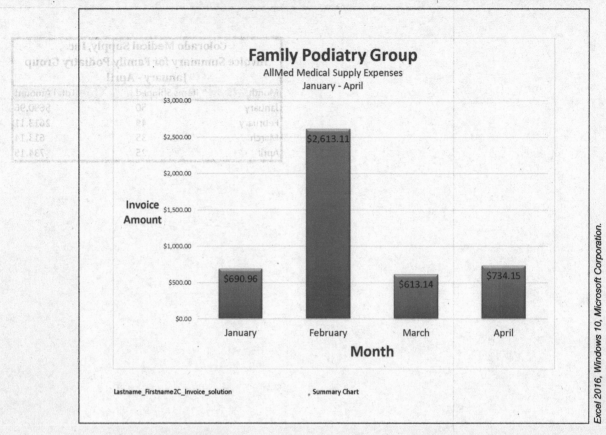

FIGURE 2.7 Project 2C Invoice

6 Create a chart.

- Create a clustered column chart showing the invoice amount for each month.
- Move the chart to a new chart sheet named **Summary Chart**.
- Format the chart to match Figure 2.7.
- In the footer, insert the codes for the file name and the sheet name.
- Move the Summary Chart worksheet so that it is after (to the right of) the Summary worksheet.

7 Check the sheets for spelling and grammar errors, and correct any errors you find. Save the workbook, and submit it as directed by your instructor.

END | You have completed Project 2C

OUTCOMES-BASED ASSESSMENTS

GO! Think   Project 2D Medical Supplies Order

Apply skills from these objectives:

1 Enter Data in a Worksheet

2 Construct and Copy Formulas and Use the SUM Function

3 Format Cells with Merge & Center and Cell Styles

4 Check Spelling in a Worksheet

5 Construct Formulas for Mathematical Operations

6 Format a Worksheet

7 Use IF Functions and Apply Conditional Formatting

8 Navigate a Workbook and Rename Worksheets

9 Edit and Format Multiple Worksheets at the Same Time

10 Create a Summary Sheet

11 Chart Data with a Pie Chart

12 Format a Pie Chart

 PROJECT FILES

For Project 2D, you will need the following file:

e2D_Medical_Supply_Orders

You will save your workbook as:

Lastname_Firstname_2D_Medical_Supply_Orders

One of your duties at Spring Pediatric Group is to keep track of medical supplies for the entire office and order them on a regular basis. You have started to create a workbook that contains a worksheet for each supplier and a summary worksheet to keep track of the total inventory value on hand. You will calculate the value of current inventory and enter an IF function to alert you when you need to reorder a particular item.

1 Create a folder in which to save your files for this project called **Medical Supply Orders.**

2 Open the file **e2D_Medical_Supply_Orders**, and save it in your **Medical Supply Orders** folder as **Lastname_Firstname_2D_Medical_Supply_Orders.**

3 Group Sheet1, Sheet2, Sheet3, and Sheet4, and then modify the grouped sheets simultaneously as follows:

- In the header, enter the text **Supply Ordering and Tracking**. In the footer, insert codes for the file name and sheet name.

- Change the orientation to Landscape.

- Format the column headings in row 8, setting fill color, bold, alignment, wrapping, and row height.

- Format the title row using merge and center, fill color, increased font size, and font color.

- In rows 3, 4, and 5, apply a fill color to the cells containing the supplier name, address, supplier number, and purchasing department information. Apply bold to the text in those three rows.

- Enter and fill a formula to calculate the inventory value for each item, referencing the cells with unit cost and quantity in stock. Only fill for those rows with supplies. If additional supplies are later added to a sheet, the formula may then be filled down further.

- Enter a function to total the inventory value. Format and border cell appropriately.

- In the Order Alert column, enter and fill an IF function to display the text ORDER when the Qty in Stock value is less than five. This will alert you to order more of each item when your current inventory falls below five. Only fill for those rows with supplies. If additional supplies are later added to a sheet, the formula may then be filled down further.

- Format using appropriate number formats, alignments, and borders.

- If necessary, adjust column widths so that each worksheet fits on one page.

- Ungroup the sheets.

4 Rename the worksheet tabs with the names of the suppliers.

(Project 2D Medical Supplies Order continues on the next page)

GO! Think **Project 2D Medical Supplies Order** (continued)

5 Enter data into the workbook as follows:

- Make up and enter at least four supplies from various suppliers.
- Fill down the formulas for each new supply.

6 Complete the Monthly Summary sheet, and add a chart to it as follows:

- In the header, insert the text **Supply Ordering and Tracking**, and insert a code for the current date. In the footer, insert codes for the file name and sheet name.
- Format the rows with similar fill color and fonts as the other worksheets, but use Portrait orientation. Set the worksheet to center horizontally on the printed page.
- Enter formulas, referencing the cells on the detail worksheets for total inventory value for each supplier.
- Enter a formula to sum the total inventory value.
- Enter and fill formulas using absolute cell referencing to calculate the percentage that each supplier's inventory represents of the total inventory.
- Format numbers appropriately.
- Create a pie chart that shows the percentage of total inventory for each supplier. Show the percentages with the slices and not in a legend.

7 Check the worksheets for spelling and grammar errors, and correct any errors you find. Save the workbook and submit it as directed by your instructor.

END | You have completed Project 2D

GO! Make It **Project 2E Inventory Database**

PROJECT FILES

For Project 2E, you will need the following files:

New blank Access database

a2E_Inventory.xlsx (Excel file)

You will save your database as:

Lastname_Firstname_2E_Inventory.accdb

PROJECT RESULTS

Apply skills from these objectives:

1 Create a Table and Define Fields in a Blank Desktop Database

2 Change the Structure of Tables and Add a Second Table

3 Create and Use a Form to Add Records

4 Create Table Relationships

5 Create a Query in Query Design

6 Sort Query Results

7 Specify Criteria in a Query

8 Specify Numeric Criteria in a Query

9 Use Compound Criteria in a Query

10 Create Calculated Fields in a Query

11 Create a Report Using the Report Wizard

12 Modify the Design of a Report

13 Close a Database and Exit Access

Lastname_Firstname_2E_Approved_Suppliers   8/11/2019

Supplier ID	Supplier Name	Street Address	City	State	ZIP	Phone	Balance Due
MF3500	Anderson Medical Supplies	5090 Washington Blvd.	Lansing	MI	48910	517-555-8765	$493.70
MF3501	G&L Medical Supplies	4321 Industrial Parkway	Philadelphia	PA	19119	215-555-3434	$1,256.00
MF3502	Karpet Speciality Supplies, Inc.	9008 Robertson Blvd.	Denver	CO	80215	303-555-7722	$836.41
MF3503	SIXA, Inc.	7893 San Mateo Boulevard	Albuquerque	NM	87123	505-555-4884	$52.11
MF3504	Goldstein & Sons Medical Supply	590 West 36th Street	New York	NY	10018	212-555-3400	$0.00
MF3505	American Medical Equipment	2400 SW Timberline Drive	Portland	OR	97225	503-555-8888	$0.00
MF3506	Dentech, Inc.	650 South Circle Drive	Colorado Springs	CO	80909	719-555-5555	$0.00

Page 1

FIGURE 2.8 Project 2E Inventory Database—Approved Suppliers Table

1 ▶ Create a folder in which to store your files for this project called **Inventory Database**.

2 ▶ From the student files that accompany this text, locate the **a2E_Inventory** Excel workbook and copy it into your **Inventory Database** folder.

3 ▶ Create a new blank desktop database named **Lastname_Firstname_2E_Inventory**, and save it in your **Inventory Database** folder.

(Project 2E Inventory Database continues on the next page)

Access 2016, Windows 10, Microsoft Corporation.

CONTENT-BASED ASSESSMENTS

GO! Make It   Project 2E Inventory Database (continued)

4 ▸ Create a table for suppliers, as shown in Figure 2.8.

• Include the following fields:

Field Name	Data Type	Description
ID	AutoNumber	Assigned by Financial Services
Supplier Name	Short Text	
Street Address	Short Text	
City	Short Text	
State	Short Text	Enter the two-letter abbreviation
ZIP	Short Text	
Phone	Short Text	
Balance Due	Currency	

• Name the table **Lastname_Firstname_2E_Approved_Suppliers**.
• Change the ID field name to **Supplier ID** and the data type to *ShortText*.
• Change the properties for the **State** field to have a *field size* of **2**.
• Change the properties for the **Balance Due** field to two decimal places.

5 ▸ Create and save a form for entering all the fields of data into this table, accepting the default layout and form name.

6 ▸ Use the form to enter data for the following seven suppliers, and then close the form.

MF3500 Anderson Medical Supplies 5090 Washington Blvd. Lansing MI 48910 517-555-8765 493.70	MF3501 G&L Medical Supplies 4321 Industrial Parkway Philadelphia PA 19119 215-555-3434 1256.00	MF3502 Karpet Specialty Supplies, Inc. 9008 Robertson Blvd. Denver CO 80215 303-555-7722 836.41
MF3503 SIXA, Inc. 7893 San Mateo Boulevard Albuquerque NM 87123 505-555-4884 52.11	MF3504 Goldstein & Sons Medical Supply 590 West 36th Street New York NY 10018 212-555-3400 0.00	MF3505 American Medical Equipment 2400 SW Timberline Drive Portland OR 97225 503-555-8888 0.00
MF3506 Dentech, Inc. 650 South Circle Drive Colorado Springs CO 80909 719-555-5555 0.00		

(Project 2E Inventory Database continues on the next page)

56   Healthcare | Chapter 2: DISCIPLINE SPECIFIC PROJECTS

PROJECT RESULTS

Item	Description	Pkg	Supplier	Supplier ID	Mfr	Unit Price	Qty in Stock
03-046-2892	Tongue Depressors, nonsterile, 500/box	BX	Anderson	MF3500	08-41556	$13.95	20
03-046-2902	Alcohol Prep Pads, 2-ply Medium, 200/box	BX	G&L	MF3501	4811172	$5.00	10
03-046-2905	Hypo Needles, Ultra-thin, 21Gx1.5", 100/bx	BX	KARPET	MF3502	0-286651	$7.50	11
03-046-2908	Cotton Tipped Applicators, 6" 1000/box	BX	SIXA	MF3503	R7200-3	$9.50	12
03-046-2913	Artiflex Nonwoven Band, 15 cm Roll	PK	G&L	MF3501	51998446	$8.95	7
07-079-9355	CaviCide Disinfectant	CA	KARPET	MF3502	0-32890	$16.95	4
07-092-4704	Post-Op Forefoot Sock, Small	EA	Anderson	MF3500	08-66453	$15.75	8
07-223-9611	Post-Op Forefoot Sock, Large	EA	SIXA	MF3503	R4519-7	$15.75	3
07-223-9788	Septicare Cleanser, 8 oz, cs/12	EA	Anderson	MF3500	08-37324	$123.00	4
07-224-2022	Post-Op Forefoot Sock, Medium	EA	SIXA	MF3503	R4519-8	$13.50	4
07-327-4002	Digital Pads, Small/Medium, 12/pk	PK	Anderson	MF3500	08-37822	$31.25	6
07-456-5099	Soft Toe Splint, Right, Medium	PK	KARPET	MF3502	0-33087	$16.95	4
07-532-1156	Toe Separator, Large 12/pk	PK	G&L	MF3501	51299005	$9.00	6
07-549-4572	Bunion Shield, Universal, 3/pk	Pk	KARPET	MF3502	0-41995	$18.00	3
07-549-6114	Soft Toe Splint, Right, Medium	PK	Anderson	MF3500	08-47992	$16.95	9
07-636-7668	Glove Polymed, Large	BX	G&L	MF3501	46202884	$8.50	11
07-888-6616	Stockinette, Cotton, 4"x25 yd	EA	KARPET	MF3502	0-32873	$32.75	8
459503-129	Procedure Mask, 50/box	BX	SIXA	MF3503	R7200-4	$11.25	15
459503-130	Sharps Container, 1qt, 12/case	CA	KARPET	MF3502	0-37881	$26.45	9
459504-327	Hypo Needles, Ultra-thin, 21Gx1.5", 100/bx	BX	KARPET	MF3502	0-279901	$16.95	6
DN0479328	Table Paper Smooth White 21"x225' 12/Ca	CA	KARPET	MF3502	0-41872	$25.00	3
DN0479329	Fabricel Pillow Cases 21 x 30", 100/Ca	CA	SIXA	MF3503	R6894-6	$32.95	12
DN0479531	Hypo Needles, Ultra-thin, 21Gx1.5", 100/bx	CA	SIXA	MF3503	R6892-4	$13.50	7
DN0479532	Specimen Cups, Sterile Wrapped, 4oz. 100/ca	CA	SIXA	MF3503	R6893-5	$24.95	8

Lastname_Firstname_2E_Supplies_Inventory — 5/22/2019

Page 1

Access 2016, Windows 10, Microsoft Corporation.

FIGURE 2.9 Project 2E Inventory Database—Supplies Inventory Table

7 Import the Excel file **a2E_Inventory** into the database as a new table, as shown in Figure 2.9.

- Use the first row as column headings.
- Allow Access to add the primary key field.
- Name the table **Lastname_Firstname_2E_Supplies_Inventory**.
- Change the primary key field to **Item**, and then delete the **ID** field.
- Change the data type for the **Unit Price** field to *Currency*, and then set the field properties to two decimal places.
- Type a description for the Supplier ID field: **Enter six-digit MF number**.
- Type a description for the **Mfr** field: **Enter manufacturer product code**.
- Save the changes to the table.
- Open both tables, and note any fields that are common to both tables. Size all the columns in each table to *Best Fit*. Save and close the tables.

8 Create a one-to-many relationship between the two tables.

- Use the **Supplier ID** field.
- Enforce referential integrity.
- Save and close the relationship.

(Project 2E Inventory Database continues on the next page)

CONTENT-BASED ASSESSMENTS

PROJECT RESULTS

Supplier ID	Supplier Name	Street Address	City	State	ZIP	Phone	Balance Due
		Lastname_Firstname_2E_Colorado_Suppliers					8/11/2019
MF3502	Karpet Speciality Supplies, Inc.	9008 Robertson Blvd.	Denver	CO	80215	303-555-7722	$836.41
MF3506	Dentech, Inc.	650 South Circle Drive	Colorado Springs	CO	80909	719-555-5555	$0.00

Page 1

FIGURE 2.10 Project 2E Inventory Database—Colorado Suppliers Query

9 Create a query to *list suppliers in Colorado*, as shown in Figure 2.10.

- Use all of the fields from the **Lastname_Firstname_2E_Approved_Suppliers** table.
- Set the criteria to display only suppliers in Colorado.
- Save the query as **Lastname_Firstname_2E_Colorado_Suppliers**. Close the query.

(Project 2E Inventory Database continues on the next page)

Access 2016, Windows 10, Microsoft Corporation.

PROJECT RESULTS

	Lastname_Firstname_2E_Quantities_in_Stock			5/22/2019

Item	Description	Pkg	Unit Price	Qty in Stock
07-223-9611	Post-Op Forefoot Sock, Large	EA	$15.75	3
DN0479328	Table Paper Smooth White 21"x225' 12/Ca	CA	$25.00	3
07-549-4572	Bunion Shield, Universal, 3/pk	Pk	$18.00	3
07-223-9788	Septicare Cleanser, 8 oz, cs/12	EA	$123.00	4
07-224-2022	Post-Op Forefoot Sock, Medium	EA	$13.50	4
07-456-5099	Soft Toe Splint, Right, Medium	PK	$16.95	4
07-079-9355	CaviCide Disinfectant	CA	$16.95	4
459504-327	Hypo Needles, Ultra-thin, 21Gx1.5", 100/bx	BX	$16.95	6
07-532-1156	Toe Separator, Large 12/pk	PK	$9.00	6
07-327-4002	Digital Pads, Small/Medium, 12/pk	PK	$31.25	6
03-046-2913	Artiflex Nonwoven Band, 15 cm Roll	PK	$8.95	7
DN0479531	Hypo Needles, Ultra-thin, 21Gx1.5", 100/bx	CA	$13.50	7
DN0479532	Specimen Cups, Sterile Wrapped, 4oz. 100/ca	CA	$24.95	8
07-092-4704	Post-Op Forefoot Sock, Small	EA	$15.75	8
07-888-6616	Stockinette, Cotton, 4"x25 yd	EA	$32.75	8
07-549-6114	Soft Toe Splint, Right, Medium	PK	$16.95	9
459503-130	Sharps Container, 1qt, 12/case	CA	$26.45	9
03-046-2902	Alcohol Prep Pads, 2-ply Medium, 200/box	BX	$5.00	10
03-046-2905	Hypo Needles, Ultra-thin, 21Gx1.5", 100/bx	BX	$7.50	11
07-636-7668	Glove Polymed, Large	BX	$8.50	11
03-046-2908	Cotton Tipped Applicators, 6" 1000/box	BX	$9.50	12
DN0479329	Fabricel Pillow Cases 21 x 30", 100/Ca	CA	$32.95	12
459503-129	Procedure Mask, 50/box	BX	$11.25	15
03-046-2892	Tongue Depressors, nonsterile, 500/box	BX	$13.95	20

Page 1

FIGURE 2.11 Project 2E Inventory Database—Quantities in Stock Query

10 ▸ Create a query to show the *quantities of supplies in stock*, as shown in Figure 2.11.
- Use **Item, Description, Pkg, Unit Price**, and **Qty in Stock** from the **Lastname_Firstname_2E_Supplies_Inventory** table.
- Sort by **Qty in Stock** in ascending order.
- Save the query as **Lastname_Firstname_2E_Quantities_in_Stock**. Close the query.

(Project 2E Inventory Database continues on the next page)

PROJECT RESULTS

Lastname_Firstname_2E_Inventory_Items_Over_$20   8/11/2019

Item	Description	Supplier	Unit Price	Qty in Stock
07-223-9788	Septicare Cleanser, 8 oz, cs/12	Anderson	$123.00	4
DN0479329	Fabricel Pillow Cases 21 x 30", 100/Ca	SIXA	$32.95	12
07-888-6616	Stockinette, Cotton, 4"x25 yd	KARPET	$32.75	8
07-327-4002	Digital Pads, Small/Medium, 12/pk	Anderson	$31.25	6
459503-130	Sharps Container, 1qt, 12/case	KARPET	$26.45	9
DN0479328	Table Paper Smooth White 21"x225' 12/Ca	KARPET	$25.00	3
DN0479532	Specimen Cups, Sterile Wrapped, 4oz. 100/case	SIXA	$24.95	8

Page 1

Access 2016, Windows 10, Microsoft Corporation.

FIGURE 2.12 Project 2E Inventory Database—Inventory Items over $20 Query

11 Create a query that shows *inventory items priced at more than $20*, as shown in Figure 2.12.

- Use **Item, Description, Pkg, Supplier, Unit Price**, and **Qty in Stock** from the **Lastname_Firstname_2E_Supplies_Inventory** table.

- Set the criteria to display only items with unit prices that are over $20.

- Sort by **Unit Price** in descending order.

- Save the query as **Lastname_Firstname_2E_Inventory_Items_Over_$20**. Close the query.

(Project 2E Inventory Database continues on the next page)

PROJECT RESULTS

Supplier	Item	Description	Pkg	Qty in Stock
Anderson	07-092-4704	Post-Op Forefoot Sock, Small	EA	8
Anderson	07-549-6114	Soft Toe Splint, Right, Medium	PK	9
Anderson	07-327-4002	Digital Pads, Small/Medium, 12/pk	PK	6
Anderson	07-223-9788	Septicare Cleanser, 8 oz, cs/12	EA	4

Lastname_Firstname_2E_Anderson_Qty_Below_15   5/22/2016

Page 1

Access 2016, Windows 10, Microsoft Corporation.

FIGURE 2.13 Project 2E Inventory Database—Anderson Qty Below 15 Query

12 Create a query that shows *inventory items from Anderson with less than 15 in stock*, as shown in Figure 2.13.

- Use **Supplier, Item, Description, Pkg, Unit Price**, and **Qty in Stock** from the **Lastname_Firstname_2E_Supplies_Inventory** table.

- Set the criteria to display only items supplied by *Anderson* and with *Qty in Stock* below 15.

- Save the query as **Lastname_Firstname_2E_Anderson_Qty_Below_15**. Close the query.

(Project 2E Inventory Database continues on the next page)

PROJECT RESULTS

Description	Supplier	Supplier ID	Unit Price	Qty in Stock	Value
Septicare Cleanser, 8 oz, cs/12	Anderson	MF3500	$123.00	4	$492.00
Fabricel Pillow Cases 21 x 30", 100/Ca	SIXA	MF3503	$32.95	12	$395.40
Tongue Depressors, nonsterile, 500/box	Anderson	MF3500	$13.95	20	$279.00
Stockinette, Cotton, 4"x25 yd	KARPET	MF3502	$32.75	8	$262.00
Sharps Container, 1qt, 12/case	KARPET	MF3502	$26.45	9	$238.05
Specimen Cups, Sterile Wrapped, 4oz. 100/case	SIXA	MF3503	$24.95	8	$199.60
Digital Pads, Small/Medium, 12/pk	Anderson	MF3500	$31.25	6	$187.50
Procedure Mask, 50/box	SIXA	MF3503	$11.25	15	$168.75
Soft Toe Splint, Right, Medium	Anderson	MF3500	$16.95	9	$152.55
Post-Op Forefoot Sock, Small	Anderson	MF3500	$15.75	8	$126.00
Cotton Tipped Applicators, 6" 1000/box	SIXA	MF3503	$9.50	12	$114.00
Hypo Needles, Ultra-thin, 21Gx1.5", 100/bx	KARPET	MF3502	$16.95	6	$101.70
Hypo Needles, Ultra-thin, 21Gx1.5", 100/bx	SIXA	MF3503	$13.50	7	$94.50
Glove Polymed, Large	G&L	MF3501	$8.50	11	$93.50
Hypo Needles, Ultra-thin, 21Gx1.5", 100/bx	KARPET	MF3502	$7.50	11	$82.50
Table Paper Smooth White 21"x225' 12/Ca	KARPET	MF3502	$25.00	3	$75.00
Soft Toe Splint, Right, Medium	KARPET	MF3502	$16.95	4	$67.80
CaviCide Disinfectant	KARPET	MF3502	$16.95	4	$67.80
Artiflex Nonwoven Band, 15 cm Roll	G&L	MF3501	$8.95	7	$62.65
Bunion Shield, Universal, 3/pk	KARPET	MF3502	$18.00	3	$54.00
Post-Op Forefoot Sock, Medium	SIXA	MF3503	$13.50	4	$54.00
Toe Separator, Large 12/pk	G&L	MF3501	$9.00	6	$54.00
Alcohol Prep Pads, 2-ply Medium, 200/box	G&L	MF3501	$5.00	10	$50.00
Post-Op Forefoot Sock, Large	SIXA	MF3503	$15.75	3	$47.25
Total					**$3,519.55**

Lastname_Firstname_2E_Current_Inventory_Value   8/13/2019

Page 1

Access 2016, Windows 10, Microsoft Corporation.

FIGURE 2.14 Project 2E Inventory Database—Current Inventory Value Query

13 Create a query to *calculate the current value of the inventory in stock*, as shown in Figure 2.14.

- Use **Description, Supplier, Supplier ID, Unit Price**, and **Qty in Stock** from the **Lastname_Firstname_2E_Supplies_Inventory** table.
- Create a calculated field named **Value** that will multiply the **Unit Price** by the **Qty in Stock** for each item.
- Sort by **Value** in descending order.
- Set the properties for the **Value** field to *Currency* with two decimal places.
- Save the query as **Lastname_Firstname_2E_Current_Inventory_Value**.
- Run the query. Add a total row to the bottom of the query result to total the **Value** field.
- Save and close the query.

(Project 2E Inventory Database continues on the next page)

GO! Make It Project 2E Inventory Database (continued)

PROJECT RESULTS

Lastname_Firstname_2E_SIXA_Current_Inventory_Value 8/13/2019

Description	Supplier ID	Unit Price	Value	Qty in Stock
Fabricel Pillow Cases 21 x 30", 100/Ca	MF3503	$32.95	$395.40	12
Specimen Cups, Sterile Wrapped, 4oz. 100/case	MF3503	$24.95	$199.60	8
Procedure Mask, 50/box	MF3503	$11.25	$168.75	15
Cotton Tipped Applicators, 6" 1000/box	MF3503	$9.50	$114.00	12
Hypo Needles, Ultra-thin, 21Gx1.5", 100/bx	MF3503	$13.50	$94.50	7
Post-Op Forefoot Sock, Medium	MF3503	$13.50	$54.00	4
Post-Op Forefoot Sock, Large	MF3503	$15.75	$47.25	3
Total			$1,073.50	

Page 1

Access 2016, Windows 10, Microsoft Corporation.

FIGURE 2.15 Project 2E Inventory Database—SIXA Current Inventory Value Query

14 Create a new query based on an existing query to show the *current value of inventory from SIXA only*, as shown in Figure 2.15.

- Open the **Lastname_Firstname_2E_Current_Inventory_Value** query and modify it.
- Enter the criteria to display only those items supplied by *SIXA*.
- Move the **Qty in Stock** column to the right of the **Value** field.
- Clear the *Show* check box for the **Supplier** field.
- Use File, Save As, and Save Object As to save this new query without overwriting the old one. Save the new query as **Lastname_Firstname_2E_SIXA_Current_Inventory_Value** and close the query.

(Project 2E Inventory Database continues on the next page)

PROJECT RESULTS

Lastname_Firstname_2E_Supplies_Inventory

Supplier	Description	Item	Pkg
Anderson			
	Digital Pads, Small/Medium, 12/	07-327-4002	PK
	Post-Op Forefoot Sock, Small	07-092-4704	EA
	Septicare Cleanser, 8 oz, cs/12	07-223-9788	EA
	Soft Toe Splint, Right, Medium	07-549-6114	PK
	Tongue Depressors, nonsterile, 5	03-046-2892	BX
G&L			
	Alcohol Prep Pads, 2-ply Medium	03-046-2902	BX
	Artiflex Nonwoven Band, 15 cm	03-046-2913	PK
	Glove Polymed, Large	07-636-7668	BX
	Toe Separator, Large 12/pk	07-532-1156	PK
KARPET			
	Bunion Shield, Universal, 3/pk	07-549-4572	Pk
	CaviCide Disinfectant	07-079-9355	CA
	Hypo Needles, Ultra-thin, 21Gx1.	459504-327	BX
	Hypo Needles, Ultra-thin, 21Gx1.	03-046-2905	BX
	Sharps Container, 1qt, 12/case	459503-130	CA
	Soft Toe Splint, Right, Medium	07-456-5099	PK
	Stockinette, Cotton, 4"x25 yd	07-888-6616	EA
	Table Paper Smooth White 21"x2	DN0479328	CA
SIXA			
	Cotton Tipped Applicators, 6" 10	03-046-2908	BX
	Fabricel Pillow Cases 21 x 30", 10	DN0479329	CA
	Hypo Needles, Ultra-thin, 21Gx1.	DN0479531	CA
	Post-Op Forefoot Sock, Large	07-223-9611	EA
	Post-Op Forefoot Sock, Medium	07-224-2022	EA
	Procedure Mask, 50/box	459503-129	BX
	Specimen Cups, Sterile Wrapped	DN0479532	CA

Thursday, August 11, 2019   Page 1 of 1

Access 2016, Windows 10, Microsoft Corporation.

FIGURE 2.16 Project 2E Inventory Database—Supplies Inventory Report

15 Using the Report Wizard, create a report as shown in Figure 2.16.

- Use **Item, Description, Supplier, Pkg**, and **Qty in Stock** from the **Lastname_Firstname_2E_Supplies_Inventory** table.
- Group by **Supplier**.
- Sort by **Description** in ascending order.
- Accept the *Stepped* and *Portrait* default settings. Finish creating the report.
- Save the report, naming it **Lastname_Firstname_2E_Supplies_Inventory_Report**.
- In Layout view, modify column widths and reposition so that all data is visible.
- Save the report.

16 Close all open objects. Close the database, and submit it as directed by your instructor.

END | You have completed Project 2E

OUTCOMES-BASED ASSESSMENTS

GO! Think   Project 2F Billing Database

PROJECT FILES

For Project 2F, you will need the following files:

a2F_Services (Excel File)

a2F_Billing (Access file)

You will save your database as:

Lastname_Firstname_2F_Billing

In this database project, you will work with a database for a medical office that includes a table with medical services and a table with patient information. You will open and edit a table, import data from Excel, create a table relationship, create and run queries, create a form, add data, and create a report.

1 Create a folder in which to store your files for this project called **Billing Database**.

2 From the student files that accompany this text, locate the **a2F_Services** Excel workbook, and copy it into your **Billing Database** folder.

3 From the student files that accompany this text, open the file **a2F_Billing**, and save it to your **Billing Database** folder as **Lastname_Firstname_2F_Billing**.

4 Enable the content, and open the **2F Patient Billing** table.

- Familiarize yourself with the data in this table.
- Move fields into a different order, rearranging them appropriately.
- Modify the table to store and format the dollar amounts appropriately.
- Save and close the table.

5 Create a new table by importing the **a2F_Services** Excel workbook.

- Use **Service Code** as the primary key.
- Save the table as **Lastname_Firstname_2F_Services**.
- Open the table. Delete any blank records. Modify the table to store and format the dollar amounts appropriately.
- Save and close the table.

6 Create relationships showing all three tables.

- Create a one-to-one relationship between the **2F Patients** and the **2F Patient Billing** tables.
- Create a one-to-many relationship between the **2F Patient Billing** table and the **Lastname_Firstname_2F_Services** table.

7 Create a form using the Form Wizard for the **2F Patients** table. Include all fields and accept all defaults. Save the form as **Lastname_Firstname_2F_Patients**.

8 Create a query that answers the question: *Which patients have had the procedure service code 00150?* Sort appropriately. Save the query with a descriptive name.

(Project 2F Billing Database continues on the next page)

Apply skills from these objectives:

1. Open and Save an Existing Database
2. Change the Structure of Tables and Add a Second Table
3. Create Table Relationships
4. Create a Query in Query Design
5. Sort Query Results
6. Specify Criteria in a Query
7. Specify Numeric Criteria in a Query
8. Use Compound Criteria in a Query
9. Create a Query Based on More Than One Table
10. Create Calculated Fields in a Query
11. Create a Form Using the Form Wizard
12. Create a Report Using the Report Wizard
13. Modify the Design of a Report
14. Close a Database and Exit Access

OUTCOMES-BASED ASSESSMENTS

9 Create a query that answers the question: *What are all the restorative and restorative major services that cost more than $100?* Sort appropriately. Save the query with a descriptive name.

10 Create a query that answers the question: *When is each patient's next appointment?* Sort appropriately. Save the query with a descriptive name.

11 Create a query with a calculated field that answers the question: *How much will each patient owe after the insurance payment?* Sort appropriately. Save the query with a descriptive name. Be sure the fields with dollar amounts are appropriately formatted. To the bottom of the query results add a total row to total the fields with dollar amounts.

12 Create a report using all the fields in the query you created showing what patients owe after insurance. Sort in appropriately. Ensure that the fields fit neatly across the page. Adjust column widths appropriately.

13 Close the database, and submit it as directed by your instructor.

END | You have completed Project 2F

CONTENT-BASED ASSESSMENTS

GO! Make It | Project 2G Lowering Blood Pressure Presentation

Apply skills from these objectives:

1. Create a New Presentation
2. Edit a Presentation in Normal View
3. Add Pictures to a Presentation
4. Print and View a Presentation
5. Edit an Existing Presentation
6. Format Slides
7. Use Slide Sorter View
8. Apply Slide Transitions
9. Format Numbered and Bulleted Lists
10. Format Objects
11. Remove Picture Backgrounds and Insert WordArt
12. Create and Format a SmartArt Graphic
13. Create and Modify Tables

 PROJECT FILES

For Project 2G, you will need the following files:

New blank PowerPoint presentation
p2G_High_Blood_Pressure.pptx
p2G_Blueberries.jpg
p2G_Cigarettes.jpg
p2G_Vegetables.jpg

You will save your presentation as:

Lastname_Firstname_2G_Blood Pressure

(Project 2G Lowering Blood Pressure Presentation continues on the next page)

PROJECT RESULTS

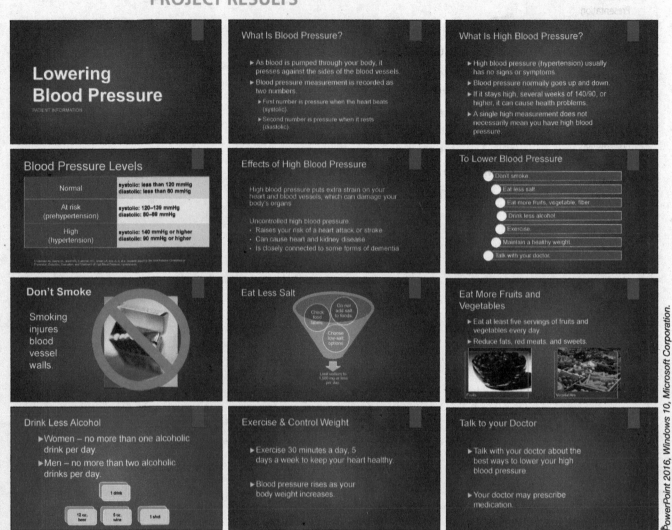

FIGURE 2.17 Project 2G Blood Pressure.

(Project 2G Lowering Blood Pressure Presentation continues on the next page)

PowerPoint 2016, Windows 10, Microsoft Corporation.

1. Create a folder for the files for this project called **Blood Pressure**.

2. Copy the **p2G** files for this project from the student project files that accompany this text into your **Blood Pressure** folder.

3. Start PowerPoint, and open a new blank presentation. Save the file in your **Blood Pressure** folder as **Lastname_Firstname_2G_Blood_Pressure**.

4. Enter **Lastname Firstname 2G Blood Pressure** as the Notes and Handouts footer.

5. Create a Title slide with WordArt, as shown in Figure 2.17.

6. Create Slide 2 using bulleted text, as shown in Figure 2.17.

7. Reuse the slides from the file **p2G_High_Blood_Pressure.pptx**. Reorder the slides, as shown in Figure 2.17.

8. Apply the *Ion* theme and the wipe transition to all slides.

9. Create a fourth slide. Insert a table, and enter the following text and format, as shown in Figure 2.17.

Blood Pressure Levels	
Normal	systolic: less than 120 mmHg
	diastolic: less than 80 mmHg
At risk (prehypertension)	systolic: 120–139 mmHg
	diastolic: 80–89 mmHg
High (hypertension)	systolic: 140 mmHg or higher
	diastolic: 90 mmHg or higher

10. Insert a footer on Slide 4 with the following source:

   • Chobanian AV, Bakris GL, Black HR, Cushman WC, Green LA, Izzo JL Jr, et al. Seventh report of the Joint National Committee on Prevention, Detection, Evaluation, and Treatment of High Blood Pressure. *Hypertension.*

11. Create the remaining slides to match Figure 2.17, using bulleted text, SmartArt, Shapes, and provided picture files.

12. Run the slide show and proofread.

13. Save the presentation, and submit it as directed by your instructor.

END | You have completed Project 2G

OUTCOMES-BASED ASSESSMENTS

GO! Think — Project 2H Patient Presentation

Apply skills from these objectives:

1 Create a New Presentation

2 Edit a Presentation in Normal View

3 Add Pictures to a Presentation

4 Print and View a Presentation

5 Format Slides

6 Apply Slide Transitions

7 Format Numbered and Bulleted Lists

8 Insert Online Pictures

9 Insert Text Boxes and Shapes

10 Format Objects

11 Remove Picture Backgrounds and Insert WordArt

12 Create and Format a SmartArt Graphic

13 Customize Slide Backgrounds and Themes

14 Animate a Slide Show

15 Create and Modify Tables

16 Create and Modify Charts

PROJECT FILES

For Project 2H, you will need the following file:

New blank PowerPoint presentation

You will save your presentation as:

Lastname_Firstname_2H_Patient

1 You are a healthcare intern at a healthcare facility. You have been asked to prepare a presentation for patients. The topic may be anything your patients must know about, such as advice for living with a particular disease or condition such as diabetes, heart disease, or gum disease, or information for those seeking a particular treatment, such as laser vein treatment or teeth whitening. Include information such as causes, symptoms, treatment options, costs, side effects, and so on.

2 Create a new folder to store your files for this project named **Patient**.

3 Create a new blank PowerPoint presentation and save it in your **Patient** folder as **Lastname_Firstname_2H_Patient**.

4 In the Notes and Handouts footer, enter your name and **2H Patient.**

5 Apply a design theme of your choice.

6 Use at least three different slide layouts.

7 Insert online pictures or photos related to your topic.

8 Use SmartArt.

9 Apply transitions to all slides, and if desired, add simple animation(s).

10 Use WordArt.

11 Apply bullets and numbering following the 6 × 6 rule. (No more than six lines of text and no more than six words in a line.)

12 Create a table or chart.

13 Insert a shape(s).

14 In the Notes pane, enter notes about the points you plan to make during the presentation.

15 Run the slide show and proofread.

16 Save the presentation, and submit it as directed by your instructor.

END | You have completed Project 2H

Discipline Specific Projects

You will complete the following discipline specific projects:

Word	GO! Make It | Project 3A Neighborhood Watch Mailing (p. 72)
	Part 1 Create a proper business letter to match visual summary.
	Use graphics, no spacing style, and character and paragraph formatting.
	Part 2 Create a newsletter to match visual summary.
	Use graphics, character and paragraph formatting, table, tab stops, footnotes, and save as a PDF.
	Part 3 Create mailing labels to match visual summary.
	Edit table, use character and paragraph formatting, and mail merge.
	Part 4 Create form letters to match visual summary.
	Use mail merge.
	GO! Think | Project 3B Seniors Mailing (p. 80)
	Part 1 Create a business letter to inform staff about senior crime prevention.
	Use graphics, no spacing style, and character and paragraph formatting.
	Part 2 Create a newsletter about senior crime prevention.
	Edit table, use graphics, character and paragraph formatting, tab stops, and save as a PDF.
	Part 3 Create mailing labels.
	Edit table, use character and paragraph formatting, and mail merge.
	Part 4 Create form letters.
	Use mail merge.
Excel	GO! Make It | Project 3C Police Calls (p. 84)
	Create a workbook to match visual summary.
	Enter data, formulas, functions; chart data; group worksheets; format; and make summary sheet.
	GO! Think | Project 3D Parking (p. 88)
	Create a Workbook to analyze prior year's parking citation revenue.
	Enter data, formulas, and functions; chart data; group worksheets; format; and make summary sheet.
Access	GO! Make It | Project 3E Training Database (p. 90)
	Work with a database to match visual summary.
	Add table, edit table structure, and join tables; create forms and reports; and create queries with compound criteria, calculated fields, and grouping.
	GO! Think | Project 3F Community Policing Database (p. 99)
	Work with a database matching officers assigned to particular apartment complexes in Colorado Springs.
	Add table, edit table structure, and join tables; create forms and reports; and create queries with compound criteria, calculated fields, and grouping.
PowerPoint	GO! Make It | Project 3G Cyber Crime Presentation (p. 100)
	Create a presentation to match visual summary.
	Format slides and work with pictures, tables, charts, WordArt, SmartArt, animation, transitions, backgrounds, and themes.
	GO! Think | Project 3H Community Presentation (p. 103)
	Create a presentation for community members.
	Format slides and work with pictures, tables, charts, WordArt, SmartArt, animation, transitions, backgrounds, and themes.

CONTENT-BASED ASSESSMENTS

Apply skills from these objectives:

1 Create a New Document from an Existing Document

2 Change Document and Paragraph Layout

3 Insert and Format Graphics

4 Use Special Character and Paragraph Formatting

5 Change and Reorganize Text

6 Use Proofing Options

7 Preview and Print a Document

PROJECT FILES

For Project 3A Administration of Justice Neighborhood Watch Mailing Part 1, you will need the following files:

w3A_Neighborhood_Watch_Letter

w3A_Neighborhood_Watch_Police_Logo

You will save your document as:

Lastname_Firstname_3A_Neighborhood_Watch_Letter

PROJECT RESULTS

COLORADO SPRINGS POLICE DEPARTMENT

2010 BEAR CREEK BLVD., COLORADO SPRINGS, CO 80903

May 15, 2019

Ms. Rebecca Patterson
4321 Cascade Avenue, Suite 200
Colorado Springs, CO 80903

Dear Ms. Patterson:

The Westside community has seen an increase in crime in recent years. Examples include home break-ins, theft, and vandalism. Some Westside citizens have expressed interest in a Neighborhood Watch program.

A Neighborhood Watch encourages neighbors to get to know each other and to pay attention and report suspicious activity regarding each other's homes and property. Citizens working with law enforcement can be very effective. Such a program can significantly reduce crime in a community and keep people safe.

You are invited to a Neighborhood Watch meeting, which will be held Sunday, February 24th at 3 p.m., at the Westside Community Center, at 2000 Bear Creek Blvd. Colorado Springs Police will be patrolling the Westside neighborhood during this time, so you need not be concerned about leaving your neighborhood vulnerable during the meeting.

At the meeting, an officer from Colorado Springs Police will provide safety and observation tips that can be implemented immediately and answer questions about Neighborhood Watch. You will learn about what is involved, and there will be an opportunity for neighbors to volunteer to be a Street Captain or Block Captain. Come and learn more about Neighborhood Watch and find out how you can help make your community a safer place.

Sincerely,

Lorenzo Rubios
Community Police Officer

Lastname_Firstname_3A_Neighborhood_Watch_Letter

Word 2016, Windows 10, Microsoft Corporation.

FIGURE 3.1 Project 3A, Part 1 Neighborhood Watch Letter

(Project 3A Part 1 Neighborhood Watch Letter continues on the next page)

1 Create a folder in which to save your files for this project. Name the folder **AJ Neighborhood Watch Mailing**.

2 From the student files that accompany this text, locate and open the file **w3A_Neighborhood_Watch_Letter**, and save it in your **AJ Neighborhood Watch Mailing** folder as **Lastname_Firstname_3A_Neighborhood_Watch_Letter**. You will modify this document to create a properly formatted business letter matching the neighborhood watch letter shown in Figure 3.1.

3 Insert a footer with the file name as a Quick Parts field in the footer.

4 Change the top margin to .5". Verify that the side and bottom margins are set to 1".

5 For the entire document, set the line spacing to single, set the paragraph spacing after to zero, and set all indents to zero.

6 In the letterhead, from your student files, insert the picture **w3A_Neighborhood_Watch_Police_Logo**. Size and position the logo in the letterhead, and set appropriate text wrapping.

7 At the top of the page, edit and align the text and format the fonts to match the letterhead at the top of the letter shown in Figure 3.1.

8 Add a border to the letterhead, as shown in Figure 3.1.

9 From the ribbon, insert the current date to match the date format shown in Figure 3.1.

10 Make corrections to the text, including size, capitalization, punctuation, and content to match the proper business letter format shown in Figure 3.1.

11 Format the letter by adding and removing blank lines to match the proper vertical spacing shown in Figure 3.1.

12 Correct any spelling or grammar errors. Preview the document and compare with Figure 3.1, making adjustments as needed.

13 Save the document in your **AJ Neighborhood Watch Mailing** folder, and submit it as directed by your instructor.

CONTENT-BASED ASSESSMENTS

Project 3A Neighborhood Watch Mailing: Part 2 Neighborhood Watch Newsletter

Apply skills from these objectives:

1 Create a New Document from an Existing Document

2 Change Document and Paragraph Layout

3 Insert a Footnote

4 Insert and Format Graphics

5 Use Special Character and Paragraph Formatting

6 Change and Reorganize Text

7 Create and Format a Table

8 Set and Modify Tab Stops

9 Use Proofing Options

10 Preview and Print a Document

11 Save a Document as a PDF

PROJECT FILES

For Project 3A Administration of Justice Neighborhood Watch Mailing Part 2, you will need the following files:

w3A_Neighborhood_Watch_Newsletter
w3A_Neighborhood_Watch_Police_Logo

You will save your documents as:

Lastname_Firstname_3A_Neighborhood_Watch_Newsletter
Lastname_Firstname_3A_Neighborhood_Watch_Newsletter_PDF

PROJECT RESULTS

Neighborhood Watch News

2010 BEAR CREEK BLVD.   **COLORADO SPRINGS POLICE DEPARTMENT**   **February**

EMERGENCY 9-1-1

NON-EMERGENCY 503-555-6034

WEST CRIME PREVENTION
Lorenzo Rubios 503-555-2893

EAST CRIME PREVENTION
Dora Rivera 503-555-5230

ELDER SAFE
Marcia Wang 503-555-6028

Burglaries Reported
Burglaries reported this month, addresses rounded to the nearest 100 block.

Residential Burglaries - No Force
7000 SW 130TH CIR
4000 NW 134TH CIR
14000 SW JENKINS RD
35000 SW LUNGER RD
18000 SW OUTLOOK CT
9000 SW CASHMA CT
7000 SW NORSE HALL RD
4000 SW 75TH AVE

Residential Burglaries - Force
4000 SW WALTON PL
8000 SW 70TH AVE
7000 SW HEXTON MOUNTAIN WY
9000 SW 71ST CIR
13000 SW BEAR MOUNTAIN RD
3000 SW ROYAL CT

Attempted Burglaries
SW SHAW ST / SW 70TH AVE
13200 SW CORNELL RD
13200 SW CORNELL RD
7000 SW 130TH CIR
7000 SW 130TH CIR
7000 SW 130TH CIR

Westside Hit by Wave of Broken Vehicle Windows
The Westside area has recently experienced a wave of broken vehicle windows. Most of the victims parked their cars on the street or in a driveway overnight and discovered damage the next morning. Colorado Springs Police are seeking the assistance from the public to keep an eye out and report suspicious activity immediately. To report a crime in progress, please call 9-1-1 right away. To report suspicious activity or a crime that has already occurred, call the non-emergency number at (503) 629-0191. If you have any suspect information regarding the wave of broken vehicle windows in our area, please call Detective Robert Ramirez in the Vehicle Crimes Unit at (503) 555-2727.

Neighborhood Watch Volunteer Trainings
You are invited to participate in informative trainings provided by the Colorado Springs Police Department especially for Neighborhood Watch volunteers. Please contact Maria Eagle to learn more about Neighborhood Watch training at (503) 555-2727. Please RSVP for each training so that we can prepare enough materials.

Date	Time	Topic
Wednesday February 16th	6:30pm	Leadership–Effective Meetings
Wednesday February 20th	6:30pm	Code Enforcement
Wednesday March 20th	6:30pm	Start Your Own Neighborhood Watch Group
Wednesday May 22nd	6:30pm	Leadership–Revitalizing Your NW Group

Fighting Crime with Your Cell Phone
You may not be aware that you can use your Cell Phone to save photo or text information to document suspicious or dangerous situations. We all occasionally find ourselves in the midst of sticky or unsafe situations. An example situation: **while walking through your parking garage, you see a suspicious vehicle you haven't seen before. Take a picture of the license plate.** Your Crime Prevention Team recommends that camera phones be used to document people, vehicles, or other unsafe situations whenever possible.

Lastname_Firstname_3A_Neighborhood_Watch_Newsletter

Word 2016, Windows 10, Microsoft Corporation.

FIGURE 3.2 Project 3A, Part 2 Neighborhood Watch Newsletter

(Project 3A Part 2 Neighborhood Watch Newsletter continues on the next page)

CONTENT-BASED ASSESSMENTS

1 From the student files that accompany this text, locate and open the file **w3A_Neighborhood_Watch_Newsletter**, and then save the file in the **AJ Neighborhood Watch Mailing** folder as **Lastname_Firstname_3A_Neighborhood_Watch_Newsletter**. You will use this file to create a one-page newsletter.

2 Make the following modifications so that the document looks like the Neighborhood Watch Newsletter shown in Figure 3.2.

3 Insert a footer with the file name as a Quick Parts field.

4 Set margins and columns to match Figure 3.2.

5 Insert the **w3A_Neighborhood_Watch_Police_Logo** picture file. Set text wrapping and size and position the logo.

6 Enter text as needed, and set tabs to match Figure 3.2.

7 Insert borders to match Figure 3.2.

8 Insert a table. Position and format to match Figure 3.2.

9 Set line and paragraph spacing, align text, and format fonts to match Figure 3.2.

10 Check the newsletter for spelling and grammar errors, and correct any errors you find. Preview the document and compare with Figure 3.2, making adjustments as needed. Ensure that the newsletter fits on one page.

11 Save the document in your **AJ Neighborhood Watch Mailing** folder.

12 Save the document again as a PDF file with the name **Lastname_Firstname_3A_Neighborhood_Watch_Newsletter_PDF** in your **AJ Neighborhood Watch Mailing** folder.

13 Submit file(s) as directed by your instructor.

CONTENT-BASED ASSESSMENTS

GO! Make It | **Project 3A Neighborhood Watch Mailing: Part 3 Neighborhood Watch Mailing Labels**

 PROJECT FILES

For Project 3A Administration of Justice Neighborhood Watch Mailing Part 3, you will need the following files:

New blank Word document
w3A_Neighborhood_Watch_Addresses

You will save your document as:

Lastname_Firstname_3A_Neighborhood_Watch_Labels

PROJECT RESULTS

Apply skills from these objectives:

1 Create Mailing Labels Using Mail Merge
2 Format a Table
3 Change Document and Paragraph Layout
4 Preview and Print a Document

Ms. Rebecca Patterson
4321 Cascade Avenue, Suite 200
Colorado Springs, CO 80903

Mr. Ernest Aguilar
50 South Nevada Avenue
Colorado Springs, CO 80903

Ms. Audra Blanch
9175 Main Street
Colorado Springs, CO 80911

Ms. Natasha Montgomery
75 Tejon Street
Colorado Springs, CO 80903

Mr. Louis Valdez
5040 Widefield Avenue
Colorado Springs, CO 80911

Ms. Jen Li Wang
900 Hancock Boulevard
Colorado Springs, CO 80909

Mr. Warren Turner-Richardson
100 Pikes Peak Avenue
Colorado Springs, CO 80903

Ms. LaKeisha Washington
39875 Blaney Road
Colorado Springs, CO 80817

Mr. Adam Meiklejohn
222 East Airport Road
Colorado Springs, CO 80909

Mr. Carter Smith
87654 Santa Fe Drive
Colorado Springs, CO 80817

Lastname_Firstname_3A_Neighborhood_Watch_Labels

Word 2016, Windows 10, Microsoft Corporation.

FIGURE 3.3 Project 3A, Part 3 Neighborhood Watch-Mailing Labels

(Project 3A Part 3 Neighborhood Watch Mailing Labels continues on the next page)

CONTENT-BASED ASSESSMENTS

1 From the student files that accompany this text, locate and copy the file **w3A_Neighborhood_Watch_Addresses** to your **AJ Neighborhood Watch Mailing** folder.

2 Starting with a new blank Word document, you will use mail merge to create a labels document that looks like the Neighborhood Watch mailing labels shown in Figure 3.3. To prevent confusion with your end results file, save this file as **Lastname_Firstname_3A_Neighborhood_Watch_Main_Labels**.

3 Use Avery US Letter, 5160 Easy Peel Address labels, which measure 1" tall by 2.63" wide.

4 The recipient data source is **3A_Neighborhood_Watch_Addresses**. Ensure that all lines fit in the label area. Preview the document, and compare with Figure 3.3, making adjustments as needed. Save the main document.

5 At the end of the merge, *Edit individual labels* to create a new file with only the label text. Save this file as **Lastname_Firstname_3A_Neighborhood_Watch_Labels** in your **AJ Neighborhood Watch Mailing** folder.

6 To the footer, add the file name as a Quick Parts field. Preview the document and, if necessary, delete blank lines or row(s) at the bottom of the table so that the entire document fits on one page (even the blank labels). Modify the bottom margin if necessary to ensure the footer will appear on the page if printed. Save this as the end results file.

7 Submit file(s) as directed by your instructor.

CONTENT-BASED ASSESSMENTS

Apply skills from these objectives:

1. Create a New Document from an Existing Document
2. Merge a Data Source and a Main Document
3. Preview and Print a Document

GO! Make It — **Project 3A Neighborhood Watch Mailing: Part 4 Neighborhood Watch Form Letters**

PROJECT FILES

For Project 3A Administration of Justice Neighborhood Watch Mailing Part 4, you will need the following files:

w3A_Neighborhood_Watch_Addresses

Lastname_Firstname_3A_Neighborhood_Watch_Letter (from Part 1 of this project)

You will save your document as:

Lastname_Firstname_3A_Neighborhood_Watch_Form_Letters

PROJECT RESULTS

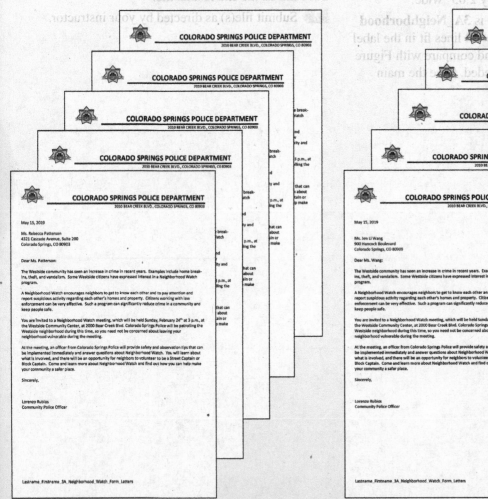

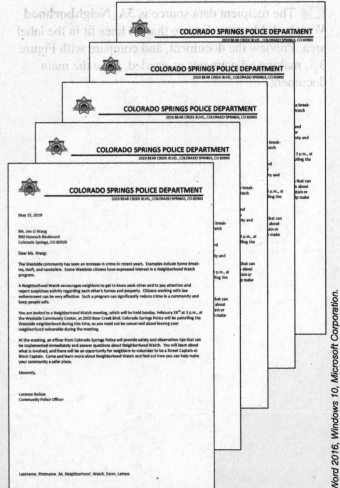

FIGURE 3.4 Project 3A, Part 4 Neighborhood Watch Form Letters

(Project 3A Part 4 Neighborhood Watch Form Letters continues on the next page)

Word 2016, Windows 10, Microsoft Corporation.

CONTENT-BASED ASSESSMENTS

1 From your **AJ Neighborhood Watch Mailing** folder, locate and open your file **Lastname_Firstname_3A_Neighborhood_Watch_Letter**. Save the file as **Lastname_Firstname_3A_Neighborhood_Watch_Main_Letter** so that you will not confuse it with your end results file. You will use mail merge to create a new document containing 10 form letters that look like the letter shown in Figure 3.4.

2 The recipient data source is **w3A_Neighborhood_Watch_Addresses**. Insert a proper business letter address block and greeting line.

3 In the footer of the main letter file, replace the field name code, typing in your *last name* and *first name* and **3A Neighborhood Watch Form Letters**. This new footer will show on each of the form letters. Save the main document file.

4 Preview the document and compare with Figure 3.4. Verify that the letters are properly formatted in the merge preview, and go back to fix as needed. Save the file as **Lastname_Firstname_3A_Neighborhood_Watch_Main_Letter**, and do not confuse it with your end results file.

5 At the end of the merge, choose to *Edit individual letters* to create a new file with the 10 letters, one on each page. Save the file with the 10 letters as **Lastname_Firstname_3A_Neighborhood_Watch_Form_Letters** in your **AJ Neighborhood Watch Mailing** folder. Save this as the end results file.

6 Submit file(s) as directed by your instructor.

END | You have completed Project 3A

OUTCOMES-BASED ASSESSMENTS

Apply skills from these objectives:

1 Create a New Document from an Existing Document

2 Change Document and Paragraph Layout

3 Insert and Format Graphics

4 Use Special Character and Paragraph Formatting

5 Change and Reorganize Text

6 Use Proofing Options

7 Preview and Print a Document

GO! Think | **Project 3B Seniors Mailing: Part 1 Seniors Letter**

 PROJECT FILES

For Project 3B Administration of Justice Seniors Mailing Part 1, you will need the following files:

New blank Word document
w3B_Police_Logo

You will save your document as:
Lastname_Firstname_3B_Seniors_Letter

You are a Colorado Springs Community police officer. You want to send a letter to senior citizens about a current local crime threat targeted at senior citizens.

1 Create a folder in which to save your files for this project called **Administration of Justice Seniors Mailing**. Open a new blank Word document, and then save the file in your **Administration of Justice Seniors Mailing** folder as **Lastname_Firstname_3B_Seniors_Letter**.

2 Add the file name to the footer as a Quick Parts field.

3 Edit and properly format a one-page business letter informing seniors about a current local crime threat. Reference the example of a properly formatted business letter in the previous project or see proper business letter requirements in Appendix A.

4 Create a letterhead for the Colorado Springs Police Department (CSPD), or reuse one created in a previous project. Include the **w3B_Police_Logo** graphic and a paragraph border in the letterhead.

5 Change the line spacing, paragraph spacing, blank lines, and text in the letter as appropriate for a properly formatted one-page business letter. Address the letter to:

Ms.	Robin	Gowda	498 West Pikes Peak Avenue	Colorado Springs	CO	80903

6 Research a current crime threat to senior citizens. Compose about 200 words of body text warning seniors, describing the threat and how to avoid it, and offering a way to get more information from the CSPD Senior Citizens Crime Prevention Unit.

7 Preview the document, and go back to adjust as needed. Adjust margins and font size appropriately to make the letter fit on one page.

8 Check the letter for spelling and grammar errors, and correct any errors you find.

9 Save the document, and submit the letter file as directed by your instructor.

OUTCOMES-BASED ASSESSMENTS

Apply skills from these objectives:

1 Create a New Document from an Existing Document
2 Change Document and Paragraph Layout
3 Insert a SmartArt Graphic
4 Insert a Footnote
5 Insert and Format Graphics
6 Use Special Character and Paragraph Formatting
7 Change and Reorganize Text
8 Create and Format a Table
9 Create and Modify Lists
10 Set and Modify Tab Stops
11 Use Proofing Options
12 Preview and Print a Document
13 Save a Document as a PDF

GO! Think | Project 3B Seniors Mailing: Part 2 Seniors Newsletter

 PROJECT FILES

For Project 3B Administration of Justice Seniors Mailing Part 2, you will need the following files:

New blank Word document
w3B_Police_Logo

You will save your documents as:

Lastname_Firstname_3B_Seniors_Newsletter
Lastname_Firstname_3B_Seniors_Newsletter_PDF

You are a community police officer. Your office publishes a one-page informational newsletter for senior citizens about crime prevention.

1 Open a new blank Word document, and then save the file in your **Administration of Justice Seniors Mailing** folder as **Lastname_Firstname_3B_Seniors_Newsletter**.

2 Do some research to find crime prevention tips for senior citizens. Keep in mind the readers of this flyer are senior citizens, so make it very easy to read, with large, clean, and clear text.

3 Add an appropriate title.

4 Insert the **w3B_Police_Logo** picture. If you wish, add additional graphical elements, but remember the priority is clear, easy reading.

5 After the title and an introductory paragraph, apply a two-column format, and use both columns to display the flyer information.

6 Apply paragraph borders. Consider possible use of lists and tables, but be careful not to clutter or make the flyer hard to read.

7 Add the file name to the footer using a Quick Parts field.

8 Check for spelling and grammar errors, and correct any errors you find.

9 For best visual results, apply document design principles: Use formatting consistently rather than randomly. Apply contrast by making titles large and bold compared with the body text. Apply design proximity by minimizing space after each title paragraph. Align all neatly.

10 Preview the document, and go back to adjust as needed. Save the document.

11 Save the document again as a PDF file with the name **Lastname_Firstname_3B_Seniors_Newsletter_PDF**.

12 Submit file(s) as directed by your instructor.

OUTCOMES-BASED ASSESSMENTS

GO! Think | **Project 3B Seniors Mailing: Part 3 Seniors Mailing Labels**

 PROJECT FILES

For Project 3B Administration of Justice Seniors Mailing Part 3, you will need the following files:

New blank Word document

w3B_Seniors_Addresses

You will save your documents as:

Lastname_Firstname_3B_Seniors_Labels

1 From the student files that accompany this text, locate and copy the file **w3B_Seniors_Addresses** to your **Administration of Justice Seniors Mailing** folder.

2 Start with a new blank Word document. To prevent confusion with the end results file, save the file as **Lastname_Firstname_3B_Seniors_Labels_Main** in your **Administration of Justice Seniors Mailing** folder.

3 Use mail merge to create labels. Your labels are Avery US Letter, 5160 Easy Peel Address labels, which are 1" tall by 2.63" wide.

4 Use the file **w3B_Seniors_Addresses** as your data source. Use Match Fields as needed to ensure complete and proper names and addresses.

5 Arrange your labels, and change spacing to ensure that all lines fit in the label area. Save the main document file.

6 After the merge is completed, *Edit individual labels* to create a new file with all the 22 labels. Save the document as **Lastname_Firstname_3B_Seniors_Labels**.

7 To the footer add the file name as a Quick Parts field. If necessary, delete blank lines or row(s) at the bottom of the table so that the entire document fits on one page (even the blank labels). Modify the bottom margin if necessary to ensure the footer will appear on the page if printed. Save this as the end results file.

8 Submit file(s) as directed by your instructor.

OUTCOMES-BASED ASSESSMENTS

<table>
<tr><td>

Apply skills from these objectives:

1 Create a New Document from an Existing Document

2 Merge a Data Source and a Main Document

3 Preview and Print a Document

</td></tr>
</table>

GO! Think | **Project 3B Seniors Mailing: Part 4 Seniors Form Letters**

 PROJECT FILES

For Project 3B Administration of Justice Seniors Mailing Part 4, you will need the following files:

Lastname_Firstname_3B_Seniors_Letter (from Part 1 of this project)

w3B_Seniors_Addresses

You will save your document as:

Lastname_Firstname_3B_Seniors_Form_Letters

1 From your **Administration of Justice Seniors Mailing** folder, locate and open your file **Lastname_Firstname_3B_Seniors_Letter**. Save the file as **Lastname_Firstname_3B_Seniors_Main_Letter** so that you will not confuse it with your end results file. Use mail merge to create properly formatted business letters.

2 In the footer of the main letter file, replace the field name code, typing in your *last name* and *first name* and **3B Seniors Form Letters**. This new footer will show on each of the form letters.

3 Use mail merge to create properly formatted business letters to each person in the data source. The data source is the student data file **w3B_Seniors_Addresses**. Use Match Fields as needed to ensure complete and proper names and addresses. Save the main document file.

4 After the merge is completed, *Edit individual letters* to create a new file with all the 22 form letters with proper business letter format.

5 Save this end results file as **Lastname_Firstname_3B_Seniors_Form_Letters**.

6 Submit file(s) as directed by your instructor.

> **END | You have completed Project 3B**

Apply skills from these objectives:

1 Enter Data in a Worksheet

2 Format Cells with Merge & Center and Cell Styles

3 Chart Data to Create a Line Chart

4 Check Spelling in a Worksheet

5 Format a Worksheet

6 Use the SUM, AVERAGE, MIN, and MAX Functions

7 Navigate a Workbook and Rename Worksheets

8 Edit and Format Multiple Worksheets at the Same Time

9 Create a Summary Sheet

GO! Make It Project 3C Police Calls

📁 PROJECT FILES

For Project 3C, you will need the following files:

e3C_Police_Calls

e3C_Police_Logo

You will save your workbook as:

Lastname_Firstname_3C_Police_Calls

PROJECT RESULTS

January Police Call Counts

	Dispatched Calls	Major Crime	Traffic Accidents	Total	Average
Precinct 1	3,998	141	176	4,315	1,438
Precinct 2	5,332	178	171	5,681	1,894
Precinct 3	5,218	210	161	5,589	1,863
Precinct 4	5,412	234	175	5,821	1,940
Precinct 5	4,568	243	162	4,973	1,658
Precinct 6	4,886	363	310	5,559	1,853
Precinct 7	2,200	84	106	2,390	797
Precinct 8	2,421	145	87	2,653	884
Total	34,035	1,598	1,348	36,981	
Average	4,254	200	169	4,623	
Lowest	2,200	84	87	2,390	
Highest	5,412	363	310	5,821	

Lastname_Firstname_3C_Police_Calls   January

Excel 2016, Windows 10, Microsoft Corporation.

FIGURE 3.5 Project 3C Police Calls

(Project 3C Police Calls continues on the next page)

1 Create a folder in which to store your files for this project called **Administration of Justice Police Calls**. From the student files that accompany this text, locate and copy the file **e3C_Police_Logo** to this folder.

2 From the student files that accompany this text, locate and open the file **e3C_Police Calls**, and then save the file in your **Administration of Justice Police Calls** folder as **Lastname_Firstname_3C_Police_Calls**. You will modify the workbook to match the worksheets shown in Figures 3.5 and 3.6.

3 Group Sheet1, Sheet2, and Sheet3, and modify the group of sheets as follows:

- Change the top margin to 3". Set the data to center horizontally on the page when printed.

- In the footer, insert the codes for the file name and the sheet name.

- In the center section of the header, insert the file **e3C_Police_Logo**.

- For the row and column heading labels, adjust column widths and row heights, and format the font, size, alignment, and wrapping to match Figure 3.5.

- Enter and fill a function to total the calls for each precinct.

- Enter and fill down AVERAGE function for each precinct to match Figure 3.5.

- Enter and fill across SUM, AVERAGE, MIN, and MAX functions for each type of police call to match Figure 3.5.

- Merge and center the title. Format the title size and color to match Figure 3.5.

- Format the cells to match Figure 3.5.

- Apply borders to match Figure 3.5.

- Ungroup the worksheets.

(Project 3C Police Calls continues on the next page)

PROJECT RESULTS

Quarter 1 Summary of Police Calls

	January	February	March	Average
Dispatched Calls	34,035	31,631	32,314	32,660
Major Crime	1,598	1,532	1,672	1,601
Traffic Accidents	1,348	1,558	1,523	1,476

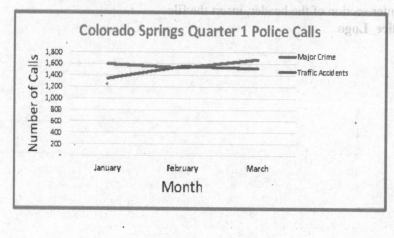

Lastname_Firstname_3C_Police_Calls   Summary

FIGURE 3.6 Project 3C Police Calls

4 Verify that the sheets are ungrouped. Rename each worksheet tab, and apply tab colors as follows:

	Sheet1	Sheet2	Sheet3	Sheet4
New tab name	January	February	March	Summary
Tab color	Red	Blue	Green	Yellow

(Project 3C Police Calls continues on the next page)

5 ▶ Modify and format the Summary worksheet as follows:

- Insert the codes for the file name and sheet name in the footer.

- In the center section of the header, insert the file **e3C_Police_Logo**.

- Change the top margin to 3", and set the worksheet to center horizontally on the printed page to match Figure 3.6.

- Enter formulas using cell references from each of the month worksheets to display the total per month of each type of call, as shown in Figure 3.6.

- On the right, enter and fill formulas to compute the average number of each type of call per month.

- Enter and format a title to match Figure 3.6.

- Adjust text format, borders and shading, row heights, and column widths to match Figure 3.6.

- Insert a line chart to visually display the monthly major crime and traffic accident calls data. Apply a Chart Layout, change the title, and size and position the chart, as shown in Figure 3.6.

6 ▶ Check the worksheets for spelling and grammar errors, and correct any errors you find. Save the workbook, and submit it as directed by your instructor.

END | You have completed Project 3C

OUTCOMES-BASED ASSESSMENTS

Apply skills from these objectives:

1 Enter Data in a Worksheet

2 Construct and Copy Formulas and Use the SUM Function

3 Format Cells with Merge & Center and Cell Styles

4 Check Spelling in a Worksheet

5 Format a Worksheet

6 Use the SUM, AVERAGE, MEDIAN, MIN, and MAX Functions

7 Navigate a Workbook and Rename Worksheets

8 Edit and Format Multiple Worksheets at the Same Time

9 Create a Summary Sheet

10 Insert Sparklines

GO! Think   Project 3D Parking

 PROJECT FILES

For Project 3D, you will need the following files:

e3D_Parking
e3D_Police_Logo

You will save your workbook as:

Lastname_Firstname_3D_Parking

You are a Colorado Springs police officer, currently assigned to the Parking Division. Your captain has asked for an analysis of the prior year's parking citation revenue. You will use quarterly data for citation count, citation fee, and dispute count to compute the revenue for each parking violation code. Your captain has asked you to combine the quarterly data and computations into a summary of parking revenue for the year.

1 Create a folder in which to store your files for this project called **Administration of Justice Parking**. From the student files that accompany this text, locate and copy the file **e3D_Police_Logo** to this folder.

2 From the student files that accompany this text, locate and open the file **e3D_Parking**, and then save it to your **Administration of Justice Parking** folder as **Lastname_Firstname_3D_Parking**.

3 Group Sheet1, Sheet2, Sheet3, and Sheet4, and modify the grouped sheets as follows:

- In the footer, insert the code for the file name and sheet name.
- Enter and fill a formula to compute the revenue for each violation code. (*Hint:* First, subtract the disputed citations from the citations count, and then multiply by the fee.)
- Enter functions to appropriately analyze the data, including at least SUM and AVERAGE. Include descriptive labels.
- Enter and format an appropriate title across the columns used. Modify column headings, if appropriate.
- Format the column headings and data, setting appropriate alignment, text wrapping, font, column width, and row height.
- Apply appropriate cell styles, borders, and fill color. Format and align all neatly.
- Make appropriate adjustments as needed so each of the grouped sheets clearly fit on one page. Ungroup the worksheets when done.

4 Rename the worksheet tabs of the ungrouped sheets as **Quarter 1 through Quarter 4**, and apply your choice of tab colors.

5 Rename the fifth sheet **Summary**, and modify as follows:

- In the footer, insert the codes for the file name and sheet name.
- Copy the violation code column from any of the quarterly worksheets to the Summary sheet.

* (Project 3D Parking continues on the next page)

OUTCOMES-BASED ASSESSMENTS

GO! Think   Project 3D Parking (continued)

- Enter and fill formulas to reference the revenue cells from the quarterly sales worksheets. Reference additional cell data as desired for analysis.

- Insert sparklines showing the revenue trend for each code quarter by quarter.

- Enter functions to appropriately summarize and analyze the data, including at least SUM and AVERAGE. Include descriptive labels.

- Enter and format an appropriate title.

- Arrange and format all neatly and professionally. Use borders, fill, cell styles, font sizes, and merge and center as appropriate.

6 Check the worksheets for spelling and grammar errors, and correct any errors you find. Ensure that the worksheets fit neatly on the printed page. Save the workbook, and submit it as directed by your instructor.

END | You have completed Project 3D

GO! Make It Project 3E Training Database

Apply skills from these objectives:

1 Open and Save an Existing Database
2 Change the Structure of Tables and Add a Second Table
3 Create a Query, Form, and Report
4 Create Table Relationships
5 Create a Query in Query Design
6 Sort Query Results
7 Specify Criteria in a Query
8 Specify Numeric Criteria in a Query
9 Use Compound Criteria in a Query
10 Create a Query Based on More Than One Table
11 Create Calculated Fields in a Query
12 Create a Form Using the Form Wizard
13 Create a Report Using the Report Wizard
14 Modify the Design of a Report
15 Save and Close a Database and Exit Access

📁 PROJECT FILES

For Project 3E, you will need the following files:

a3E_Training.accdb
a3E_Station8_Staff.xlsx

You will save your database as:

Lastname_Firstname_3E_Training.accdb

PROJECT RESULTS

EMP ID	**LAST NAME**	**FIRST NAME**	**SHIFT**	**RNK**	**SERV YRS**	**SALARY**	**ADDRESS**	**CITY**	**STATE**	**ZIP**	**PHONE**
13550	Talbot	Andrew	2	PM	3	$48,750.00	45 West Manitou Avenue	Colorado Springs	CO	80905	719-555-1523
13660	Blanco	Martin	2	PM	2	$48,523.00	755 East El Pomar Drive	Colorado Springs	CO	80915	719-555-1287
13778	Winters	Steven	2	1C	4	$43,560.00	189 Lake Drive	Colorado Springs	CO	80906	719-555-1298
13892	Blankenship	Thomas	1	2C	3	$41,968.00	2589 East Constitution	Colorado Springs	CO	80916	719-555-1237
13994	Martinez	Kevin	1	PM	11	$51,472.00	2626 East Woodmen Rd.	Colorado Springs	CO	80918	719-555-5123
16290	McFerraro	Nathan	2	DR	7	$51,826.00	1589 Centennial Blvd.	Colorado Springs	CO	80911	719-555-1258
16333	Washington	Terrell	1	1C	7	$44,041.60	1036 Highway 83	Colorado Springs	CO	80922	719-555-4223
18863	Smith	Randall	1	BC	18	$85,513.60	1234 Chapel Hills	Colorado Springs	CO	80920	719-555-9982
19864	Miller	Anthony	1	DR	8	$52,176.00	5697 W. Briargate Blvd.	Colorado Springs	CO	80919	719-555-8793
45765	Montella	Will	2	2C	5	$44,825.00	25 East Colorado Avenue	Colorado Springs	CO	80902	719-555-7654
45891	Cordova	Richard	1	1C	5	$44,041.60	13 East Cheyenne Mtn. Road	Colorado Springs	CO	80915	719-555-2890
65233	O'Malley	Martin	1	DR	6	$50,176.00	2525 W. Rockrimmon Blvd.	Colorado Springs	CO	80918	719-555-5992
65523	Warners	Ted	2	DR	6	$50,176.00	45 South Cascade	Colorado Springs	CO	80910	719-555-1789
82543	Apuro	Daniel	2	LT	9	$53,892.00	189 Rampart Range Road	Colorado Springs	CO	80922	719-555-1898
82633	Cunningham	Cheryl	1	LT	10	$54,582.40	29 West Pikes Peak	Colorado Springs	CO	80914	719-555-3124
82636	Baca	David	1	CP	15	$59,248.00	1289 South Circle	Colorado Springs	CO	80910	719-555-2336
82640	Roccos	Adam	2	CP	14	$58,525.00	8926 Garden of the Gods Road	Colorado Springs	CO	80915	719-555-1833
89257	Baker	Samantha	1	PM	8	$51,472.00	5672 North Academy	Colorado Springs	CO	80920	719-555-3326

Lastname_Firstname_3E_Station_8_Staffing   8/18/2019

Page 1

Access 2016, Windows 10, Microsoft Corporation.

FIGURE 3.7 Project 3E Training Database—Station 8 Staffing Table

1 Create a new folder called **Training Database** in which to store the files for this project.

2 From the student data files that accompany this text, locate and copy the Excel file, **a3E_Station8_Staff.xlsx**, to your **Training Database** folder.

3 From the student data files that accompany this text, open **a3E_Training.accdb**, and save the database in your **Training Database** folder as **Lastname_Firstname_3E_Training**. Enable the content. Open the **3E Station 8 Training** table, and become familiar with its contents.

(Project 3E Training Database continues on the next page)

4 ▸ Create a new table by importing the **a3E_Station8_Staff** Excel workbook.

- Use the first row as column headings.
- Use the **EMP ID** field as the primary key.
- Name the table **Lastname_Firstname_3E_Station_8_Staffing**.

5 ▸ Modify the **Lastname_Firstname_3E_Station_8_Staffing** table structure to match Figure 3.7.

- Move the **SHIFT** field before the **RNK** field.
- Add a description for the **SERV YRS** that says **Total Years with Department**.
- Change the properties for the **RNK** field to have a field size of 2. Save and close the table.

6 ▸ Create a form for working with the data in the **Lastname_Firstname_3E_Station_8_Staffing** table using the Form Wizard.

- Accept the default settings.
- Save it as **Lastname_Firstname_3E_Station_8_Staffing**. Close the form.

7 ▸ Create a one-to-one relationship between the two tables.

- Use the **EMP ID** field.
- Enforce referential integrity.
- Size the tables so all fields are visible.
- Save and close the relationship.

8 ▸ Open the **Lastname_Firstname_3E_Station_8_Staffing** table. You will see a plus sign or expand symbol to the left of the first field. When you click on the plus sign, you will see the trainings from the **3E Station 8 Training** table for that employee. Open the **3E Station 8 Training** table. You will see the plus sign or expand symbol to the left of the first field. When you click on the plus sign, you will see the data for each employee. Close all open objects.

(Project 3E Training Database continues on the next page)

PROJECT RESULTS

Lastname_Firstname_3E_Staff_RNK_YRS_SHIFT					8/18/2019

EMP ID	LAST NAME	FIRST NAME	RNK	SERV YRS	SHIFT
13778	Winters	Steven	1C	4	2
45891	Cordova	Richard	1C	5	1
16333	Washington	Terrell	1C	7	1
13892	Blankenship	Thomas	2C	3	1
45765	Montella	Will	2C	5	2
18863	Smith	Randall	BC	18	1
82640	Roccos	Adam	CP	14	2
82636	Baca	David	CP	15	1
65523	Warners	Ted	DR	6	2
65233	O'Malley	Martin	DR	6	1
16290	McFerraro	Nathan	DR	7	2
19864	Miller	Anthony	DR	8	1
82543	Apuro	Daniel	LT	9	2
82633	Cunningham	Cheryl	LT	10	1
13660	Blanco	Martin	PM	2	2
13550	Talbot	Andrew	PM	3	2
89257	Baker	Samantha	PM	8	1
13994	Martinez	Kevin	PM	11	1

Page 1

Access 2016, Windows 10, Microsoft Corporation.

FIGURE 3.8 Project 3E Training Database—Staff RNK YRS SHIFT Query

9 ▶ Create a query listing all the station staff members and their rank, years of service, and shift to match Figure 3.8.

- Show **EMP ID**, **LAST NAME**, **FIRST NAME**, **RNK**, **SERV YRS**, and **SHIFT**.
- Sort by **RNK** in ascending order and by **SERV YRS** in ascending order.
- Save the query as **Lastname_Firstname_3E_Staff_RNK_YRS_SHIFT**.

(Project 3E Training Database continues on the next page)

PROJECT RESULTS

Lastname_Firstname_3E_Shift_1   8/20/2019

EMP ID	LAST NAME	FIRST NAME	RNK	SHIFT
82636	Baca	David	CP	1
89257	Baker	Samantha	PM	1
13892	Blankenship	Thomas	2C	1
45891	Cordova	Richard	1C	1
82633	Cunningham	Cheryl	LT	1
13994	Martinez	Kevin	PM	1
19864	Miller	Anthony	DR	1
65233	O'Malley	Martin	DR	1
18863	Smith	Randall	BC	1
16333	Washington	Terrell	1C	1

Page 1

Access 2016, Windows 10, Microsoft Corporation.

FIGURE 3.9 Project 3E Training Database—Shift 1 Query

10 Create a query to match Figure 3.9 that answers the question, *Which employees work shift 1?*

- Show **EMP ID, LAST NAME, FIRST NAME, RNK**, and **SHIFT**.
- Sort by **LAST NAME** in ascending order.
- Save the query as **Lastname_Firstname_3E_Shift_1** and then close the query.

(Project 3E Training Database continues on the next page)

PROJECT RESULTS

	Lastname_Firstname_3E_Staff_7_or_More_Yrs			8/16/2019
LAST NAME	**FIRST NAME**	**RNK**	**SERV YRS**	**SALARY**
Washington	Terrell	1C	7	$44,041.60
Smith	Randall	BC	18	$85,513.60
Baca	David	CP	15	$59,248.00
Roccos	Adam	CP	14	$58,525.00
Miller	Anthony	DR	8	$52,176.00
McFerraro	Nathan	DR	7	$51,826.00
Cunningham	Cheryl	LT	10	$54,582.40
Apuro	Daniel	LT	9	$53,892.00
Martinez	Kevin	PM	11	$51,472.00
Baker	Samantha	PM	8	$51,472.00

Page 1

Access 2016, Windows 10, Microsoft Corporation.

FIGURE 3.10 Project 3E Training Database—Staff 7 or More Yrs Query

11 Create a query to match Figure 3.10 that answers the question, *Which firefighters have seven or more years of service?*

- Show **LAST NAME, FIRST NAME, RNK, SERV YRS**, and **SALARY**.
- Sort by **RNK** in ascending order and **SERV YRS** in descending order.
- Save the query as **Lastname_Firstname_3E_Staff_7_or_More_Yrs**.

(Project 3E Training Database continues on the next page)

PROJECT RESULTS

Lastname_Firstname_3E_DR_and_PM_More_Than_7yrs   8/16/2019

LAST NAME	FIRST NAME	RNK	SERV YRS	SALARY
Martinez	Kevin	PM	11	$51,472.00
Miller	Anthony	DR	8	$52,176.00
Baker	Samantha	PM	8	$51,472.00

Page 1

Access 2016, Windows 10, Microsoft Corporation.

FIGURE 3.11 Project 3E Training Database—DR and PM More than 7 Yrs Query

12 Create a query to match Figure 3.11 that answers the question, *Which DRs and PMs have more than seven years of service?*

- Show **LAST NAME, FIRST NAME, RNK, SERV YRS**, and **SALARY**.
- Sort by **SERV YRS** in descending order and **SALARY** in descending order.
- Save the query as **Lastname_Firstname_3E_DR_and_PM_More_Than_7 yrs**, and then close the query.

(Project 3E Training Database continues on the next page)

PROJECT RESULTS

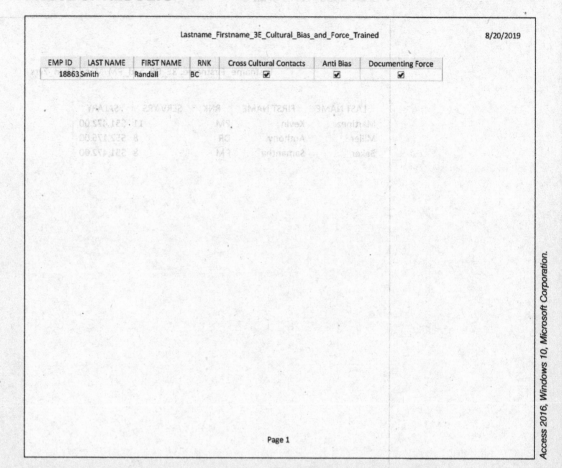

FIGURE 3.12 Project 3E Training Database—Cultural, Bias, and Force Trained Query

> 13 Create a query to match Figure 3.12, using both tables that answers the following
> question: *Which employees have all three trainings: Cross Cultural Contacts, Anti Bias,
> and Documenting Force?*
>
> - Show **EMP ID, LAST NAME, FIRST NAME, RNK, Cross Cultural
>   Contacts, Anti Bias,** and **Documenting Force**.
> - Save the query as **Lastname_Firstname_3E_Cultural,_Bias,_and Force_Trained**
>   and then close the query.

(Project 3E Training Database continues on the next page)

PROJECT RESULTS

EMP ID	LAST NAME	FIRST NAME	RNK	SERV YRS	SALARY	RAISE	NEW SALARY
					Lastname_Firstname_3E_New_Salaries		8/16/2019
82640	Roccos	Adam	CP	14	$58,525.00	$2,048.38	$60,573.38
13550	Talbot	Andrew	PM	3	$48,750.00	$1,706.25	$50,456.25
19864	Miller	Anthony	DR	8	$52,176.00	$1,826.16	$54,002.16
82633	Cunningham	Cheryl	LT	10	$54,582.40	$1,910.38	$56,492.78
82543	Apuro	Daniel	LT	9	$53,892.00	$1,886.22	$55,778.22
82636	Baca	David	CP	15	$59,248.00	$2,073.68	$61,321.68
13994	Martinez	Kevin	PM	11	$51,472.00	$1,801.52	$53,273.52
65233	O'Malley	Martin	DR	6	$50,176.00	$1,756.16	$51,932.16
13660	Blanco	Martin	PM	2	$48,523.00	$1,698.31	$50,221.31
16290	McFerraro	Nathan	DR	7	$51,826.00	$1,813.91	$53,639.91
18863	Smith	Randall	BC	18	$85,513.60	$2,992.98	$88,506.58
45891	Cordova	Richard	1C	5	$44,041.60	$1,541.46	$45,583.06
89257	Baker	Samantha	PM	8	$51,472.00	$1,801.52	$53,273.52
13778	Winters	Steven	1C	4	$43,560.00	$1,524.60	$45,084.60
65523	Warners	Ted	DR	6	$50,176.00	$1,756.16	$51,932.16
16333	Washington	Terrell	1C	7	$44,041.60	$1,541.46	$45,583.06
13892	Blankenship	Thomas	2C	3	$41,968.00	$1,468.88	$43,436.88
45765	Montella	Will	2C	5	$44,825.00	$1,568.88	$46,393.88
Total						$32,716.89	$967,485.09

Page 1

FIGURE 3.13 Project 3E Training Database—New Salaries Query

14 Create a query to match Figure 3.13 that answers the question, *What will the new salaries total after a 3.5% cost-of-living adjustment?*

- Show the **EMP ID**, **LAST NAME**, **FIRST NAME**, **RNK**, **SERV YRS**, and **SALARY**.
- Create a calculated field **RAISE** that shows a raise by multiplying **.035** by the **SALARY**.
- Create another calculated field **NEW SALARY** that shows the new salary amount by adding the **SALARY** and **RAISE** fields.
- Format the new fields in *Currency*.
- Sort by **LAST NAME** in ascending order.
- After running the query, add a total row to the bottom of the results to total the **RAISE** and **NEW SALARY** fields.
- Save the query as **Lastname_Firstname_3E_New_Salaries**, and then close the query.

(Project 3E Training Database continues on the next page)

PROJECT RESULTS

Lastname_Firstname_3E_New_Salaries					
LAST NAME	RNK	SERV YRS	SALARY	RAISE	NEW SALARY
Apuro	LT	9	$53,892.00	$1,886.22	$55,778.22
Baca	CP	15	$59,248.00	$2,073.68	$61,321.68
Baker	PM	8	$51,472.00	$1,801.52	$53,273.52
Blanco	PM	2	$48,523.00	$1,698.31	$50,221.31
Blankenship	2C	3	$41,968.00	$1,468.88	$43,436.88
Cordova	1C	5	$44,041.60	$1,541.46	$45,583.06
Cunningham	LT	10	$54,582.40	$1,910.38	$56,492.78
Martinez	PM	11	$51,472.00	$1,801.52	$53,273.52
McFerraro	DR	7	$51,826.00	$1,813.91	$53,639.91
Miller	DR	8	$52,176.00	$1,826.16	$54,002.16
Montella	2C	5	$44,825.00	$1,568.88	$46,393.88
O'Malley	DR	6	$50,176.00	$1,756.16	$51,932.16
Roccos	CP	14	$58,525.00	$2,048.38	$60,573.38
Smith	BC	18	$85,513.60	$2,992.98	$88,506.58
Talbot	PM	3	$48,750.00	$1,706.25	$50,456.25
Warners	DR	6	$50,176.00	$1,756.16	$51,932.16
Washington	1C	7	$44,041.60	$1,541.46	$45,583.06
Winters	1C	4	$43,560.00	$1,524.60	$45,084.60

August 18, 2019

Page 1 of 1

Access 2016, Windows 10, Microsoft Corporation.

FIGURE 3.14 Project 3E Training Database—New Salaries Report

15 Create a report using the Report Wizard to match Figure 3.14.
- Use the **Lastname_Firstname_3E_New_Salaries** query.
- Do not include the **FIRST NAME** field.
- Do not group.
- Sort by **LAST NAME** in ascending order.
- Use *Tabular* layout and *Landscape* orientation.
- Save the report as **Lastname_Firstname_3E_New_Salaries**.

16 Modify the report in Layout view.
- Delete the **EMP ID** field.
- Widen and reposition the fields so that the report looks good and all data is visible on one page.
- Center the column headings. Center the data in all the columns *except* **LAST NAME**. Save and close the report.

17 Close the database, and submit it as directed by your instructor.

END | You have completed Project 3E

OUTCOMES-BASED ASSESSMENTS

GO! Think Project 3F Community Policing Database

Apply skills from these objectives:

1 Open and Save an Existing Database

2 Change the Structure of Tables and Add a Second Table

3 Create Table Relationships

4 Create a Query in Query Design

5 Sort Query Results

6 Specify Criteria in a Query

7 Specify Numeric Criteria in a Query

8 Create a Query Based on More Than One Table

9 Create a Form Using the Form Wizard

10 Create a Report Using the Report Wizard

11 Modify the Design of a Report

12 Save and Close a Database and Exit Access

 PROJECT FILES

For Project 3F, you will need the following files:

a3F_Community_Policing.accdb (Access database)
a3F_Apartments.xlsx (Excel file)

You will save your database as:

Lastname_Firstname_3F_Community_Policing.accdb

You are a police officer currently assigned to community policing coordination. Your captain has asked you to work with database matching officers assigned to particular apartment complexes in Colorado Springs.

1 Create a new folder called **Community Policing Database** in which to store the files for this project.

2 Locate and copy the Excel file **a3F_Apartments** to your **Community Policing Database** folder.

3 From the student data files that accompany this text, open **a3F_Community_Policing.accdb**, and save it in your **Community Policing Database** folder as **Lastname_Firstname_3F_Community_Policing**. Enable the content.

4 In the **Lastname_Firstname_3F_Community_Policing** database, create a new table by importing the Excel file **a3F_Apartments**. Save the table as **Lastname_Firstname_3F_Apartments**.

5 In the **Lastname_Firstname_3F_Community_Policing** database, create a new table called **Lastname Firstname 3F Assignments** in which to list the officers assigned as community police officers to the different apartment complexes. Include assignment start and end date fields and fields that correspond with the **EMP ID** field in the Staff table and the **Business ID** field in the Apartments table.

6 Create a form for the **Lastname_Firstname_3F_Assignments** table. Using the form, assign at least one officer to each apartment complex. Enter various start and end dates.

- Leave some end dates blank to represent current assignments.

7 Create relationships between the three tables. Save the relationship.

8 Create and save queries to answer the following questions. Include appropriate fields, sort, and format fields appropriately. Save with descriptive names.

- *What is the name and street address for each apartment building? Who is the contact person for each building, and what is the phone number?*
- *Which officers have salaries of more than $50,000 per year?*
- *List, for all current assignments, the apartment name and officer name.*
- *Which officers are assigned to apartment complexes that are not in Colorado Springs?*

9 Create an officer assignments report that displays the business IDs, business name, and officer's name. Widen and reposition columns as needed so that all data is visible. Save the report with the default name.

10 Save and close the database. Submit it as directed by your instructor.

END | You have completed Project 3F

CONTENT-BASED ASSESSMENTS

Apply skills from these objectives:

1 Create a New Presentation
2 Edit a Presentation in Normal View
3 Add Pictures to a Presentation
4 Print and View a Presentation
5 Edit an Existing Presentation
6 Format Slides
.7 Use Slide Sorter View
8 Apply Slide Transitions
9 Format Numbered and Bulleted Lists
10 Format Objects
11 Create and Format a SmartArt Graphic
12 Create and Modify Tables

GO! Make It Project 3G Cyber Crime Presentation

 PROJECT FILES

For Project 3G, you will need the following files:

New blank PowerPoint presentation
p3G_Contact_Information.pptx
p3G_Calendar.jpg
p3G_Police_Logo.jpg

You will save your presentation as:

Lastname_Firstname_3G_Cyber_Crime

(Project 3G Cyber Crime Presentation continues on the next page)

PROJECT RESULTS

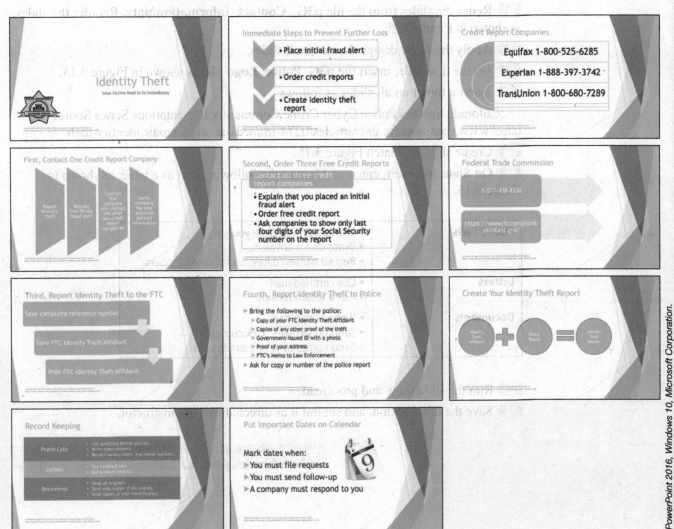

FIGURE 3.15 Project 3G Cyber Crime Presentation

PowerPoint 2016, Windows 10, Microsoft Corporation.

1 Your boss is planning to make a series of presentations to community members about cyber crime. As an intern with the Colorado Springs Police, you have been asked to create a brief visual PowerPoint presentation about immediate steps to take following an identity theft to match Figure 3.15.

2 Create a folder for the files for this project called **Cyber Crime**.

3 Copy the files **p3G_Contact_Information.pptx, p3G_Calendar.jpg**, and **p3G_Police_Logo.jpg** from the student project files that accompany this text into your **Cyber Crime** folder.

4 Start PowerPoint, and open a new blank presentation. Save the file in your **Cyber Crime** folder as **Lastname_Firstname_3G_ Cyber_Crime**.

(Project 3G Cyber Crime Presentation continues on the next page)

CONTENT-BASED ASSESSMENTS

5️⃣ In the Notes and Handouts footer, enter your name and **3G Cyber Crime**.

6️⃣ Reuse the slides from the file **p3G_ Contact_Information.pptx**. Reorder the slides, as shown in Figure 3.15.

7️⃣ Apply the *Facet* design theme on all slides.

8️⃣ On the title slide, insert the **p3G_Police_Logo** file, as shown in Figure 3.15.

9️⃣ Insert a footer on all slides as follows:

Colorado Springs Police Cyber Crime Community Presentations Series Source: http://www.consumer.ftc.gov/articles/0274-immediate-steps-repair-identity-theft

🔟 Create slides to match Figure 3.15.

11 On Slide 10, insert, enter, and format the following text as a table, as shown in Figure 3.15.

Phone Calls	• List questions before you call. • Write down answers. • Record names, dates, and phone numbers.
Letters	• Use certified mail. • Get a return receipt.
Documents	• Keep all originals. • Send only copies of documents. • Send copies of your identification.

12 Run the slide show and proofread.

13 Save the presentation, and submit it as directed by your instructor.

END | You have completed Project 3G

OUTCOMES-BASED ASSESSMENTS

Apply skills from these objectives:

1 Create a New Presentation

2 Edit a Presentation in Normal View

3 Add Pictures to a Presentation

4 Print and View a Presentation

5 Format Slides

6 Apply Slide Transitions

7 Format Numbered and Bulleted Lists

8 Insert Online Pictures

9 Insert Text Boxes and Shapes

10 Format Objects

11 Create and Format a SmartArt Graphic

12 Customize Slide Backgrounds and Themes

13 Animate a Slide Show

14 Create and Modify Tables

15 Create and Modify Charts

GO! Think | Project 3H Community Presentation

 PROJECT FILES

For Project 3H, you will need the following file:

New blank PowerPoint presentation

You will save your presentation as:

Lastname_Firstname_3H_Community

You are a summer intern at an Administration of Justice agency. You have been asked to prepare a presentation for community members. The topic may be anything your citizens must know about, such as talking to children about terrorism, dealing with a traffic ticket, what to do if a loved one is in jail, and so on. As you prepare your slides, follow these steps:

1 Create a new folder for your files for this project, and name it **Community**.

2 Create a new blank PowerPoint presentation file. Save the file in your **Community** folder as **Lastname_Firstname_3H_Community**.

3 In the footer for Notes and Handouts, display *your name* and **3H** Community.

4 Insert the following footer on the slides: **Presented by** Firstname Lastname.

5 Apply an appropriate design theme. Customize the design as desired.

6 Use at least three different slide layouts. Follow the 6 × 6 rule on slides with bulleted lists. (No more than six lines of text and no more than six words in a line.)

7 Clearly identify any sources used.

8 Insert at least one Online Picture or a photo related to your topic.

9 Insert SmartArt on at least one slide.

10 Apply transitions to all slides and, if desired, add simple animation(s).

11 Apply bullets and numbering on at least one slide.

12 Create a table *or* chart.

13 Insert a shape on one or more slides.

14 In the Notes pane, enter notes about what to say during the presentation.

15 Run the slide show and proofread.

16 Save the presentation and submit it as directed by your instructor.

END | You have completed Project 3H

Discipline Specific Projects

You will complete the following discipline specific projects:

Word	**GO! Make It | Project 4A Client Mailing (p. 106)**

GO! Make It \| Project 4A Client Mailing (p. 106)

Part 1 Create a proper business letter to match visual summary.
Use graphics, text box, no spacing style, and character and paragraph formatting.

Part 2 Create a motion to match visual summary.
Use graphics, character and paragraph formatting, table, footnotes, save as a PDF, and track changes.

Part 3 Create mailing labels to match visual summary.
Edit table. Use character and paragraph formatting, and mail merge.

Part 4 Create form letters to match visual summary.
Use mail merge.

GO! Think \| Project 4B Legal Stock Mailing (p. 115)

Part 1 Create a business letter to send stock documents to investors.
Use graphics, text box, no spacing style, and character and paragraph formatting.

Part 2 Create an MLA paper about digital copyright.
Use paragraph formatting, page numbering, footnotes, citations, Source Manager, and save as a PDF.

Part 3 Create mailing labels.
Edit table. Use character and paragraph formatting, and mail merge.

Part 4 Create form letters.
Use mail merge.

Excel

GO! Make It \| Project 4C Stockholder Ledger (p. 120)

Create a workbook to match visual summary.
Enter data, formulas, and functions; chart data; group worksheets, format, and make summary sheet.

GO! Think \| Project 4D Billable Hours (p. 125)

Create a workbook to keep track of billable hours for specific cases.
Enter data, formulas, and functions; chart data; group worksheets, format, and make summary sheet.

Access

GO! Make It \| Project 4E Caseload Database (p. 127)

Work with a database to match visual summary.
Add table, edit table structure, and join tables; create forms and reports; create queries with compound criteria, calculated field, and grouping.

GO! Think \| Project 4F Stockholders Database (p. 138)

Work with a stockholders database.
Add table, edit table structure, and join tables; create forms and reports; and create queries with compound criteria, calculated field, and grouping.

PowerPoint

GO! Make It \| Project 4G Jury Selection (p. 140)

Create a presentation to match visual summary.
Format slides, work with pictures, table, chart, WordArt, SmartArt, animation, transition, backgrounds, and themes.

GO! Think \| Project 4H Community Presentation (p. 144)

Create a presentation for a community service workshop on a legal topic.
Format slides, work with pictures, table, chart, WordArt, SmartArt, animation, transition, backgrounds, and themes.

Apply skills from
these objectives:

**Apply skills from
these objectives:**

1 Create a New
Document from an
Existing Document

2 Change Document and
Paragraph Layout

3 Insert and Format
Graphics

4 Use Special Character
and Paragraph
Formatting

5 Change and Reorganize
Text

6 Insert and Modify Text
Boxes and Shapes

7 Create and Format a
Table

8 Use Proofing Options

9 Preview and Print a
Document

GO! Make It | **Project 4A Client Mailing:
Part 1 Client Letter**

📁 PROJECT FILES

For Project 4A Client Mailing Part 1, you will need the following files:

w4A_Client_Letter

w4A_Flag

You will save your document as:

Lastname_Firstname_4A_Client_Letter

PROJECT RESULTS

**Trusty, Loyal,
& True, LLC**

Attorneys at Law
200 Cascade Avenue, Suite 400
Colorado Springs, CO 80903
Phone Number: 719-555-5555
FAX: 719-555-5556
E-mail: tltlaw@url.com

February 15, 2019

Mrs. Janelle Deer
707 Highlands Trail
Colorado Springs, CO 80906

Dear Mrs. Deer:

It was a pleasure to meet with you last month to review your role in the class action lawsuit against
BADCO Insurance. As we discussed, the testimony of our eyewitness, Lt. Steven Smart, will be critical to
a favorable ruling in our case.

Lt. Smart is serving our country in the Middle East, so it will not be possible for him to personally appear
in court on December 15. Therefore, we are requesting a MOTION FOR ABSENTEE TESTIMONY, which
will allow him to testify by telephone. The time frame for processing this motion is as follows:

Prepare Motion for Absentee Testimony	March 17
Receive Signed Motion from Client	March 27
File Motion in District Court	April 1
Take Absentee Testimony	December 15

As always, call me any time you have questions.

Sincerely,

Barbara Loyal, B.A., J.D.

Enclosure

Lastname_Firstname_4A_Client_Letter

Word 2016, Windows 10, Microsoft Corporation.

FIGURE 4.1 Project 4A, Part 1 Client Letter

(Project 4A Part 1 Client Letter continues on the next page)

CONTENT-BASED ASSESSMENTS

1 Create a folder in which to save your files for this project called **Legal Client Mailing**.

2 From the student files that accompany this text, locate and copy the file **w4A_Flag** to your **Legal Client Mailing** folder.

3 From the student files that accompany this text, locate and open the file **w4A_Client_Letter**, and then save the file in your **Legal Client Mailing** folder as **Lastname_Firstname_4A_Client_Letter**. Make the following modifications so that the document looks like the one shown in Figure 4.1.

4 Insert a footer with the file name as a Quick Parts field in the left section of the footer. Change the footer font if necessary to match the body of the letter.

5 Change the top margin to .5". Verify that the side and bottom margins are set to 1".

6 For the entire document, verify that the line spacing is set to single, the paragraph spacing after is set to zero, and all indents are set to zero.

7 Insert the **w4A_Flag** picture in the letterhead. Set the picture style, wrapping, and position as shown in Figure 4.1. Crop edges if needed.

8 Align and format the text *Trusty, Loyal, & True, LLC* to match the letterhead at the top of the letter shown in Figure 4.1. Add space before the paragraph if needed. Use a text box and a small font for the contact information. Add a top border to the blank line below the letterhead as shown in Figure 4.1.

9 From the ribbon, insert the current date to match the date format shown in Figure 4.1. Enter appropriate year numbers for all dates in the letter.

10 Format the letter by adding and removing blank lines, adjusting vertical spacing to match the properly formatted business letter shown in Figure 4.1.

11 On the second blank line after the sentence, *The time frame for processing this motion is as follows:*, insert a table as shown in Figure 4.1.

12 Check your document for spelling and grammar errors, and correct any errors you find. Preview the document, and compare with Figure 4.1, making adjustments as needed.

13 Save your document, and submit it as directed by your instructor.

CONTENT-BASED ASSESSMENTS

Apply skills from these objectives:

1 Create a New Document from an Existing Document
2 Edit a Document Using Track Changes
3 Create a Table
4 Change and Reorganize Text
5 Create and Modify Lists
6 Insert Footnotes
7 Use Special Character and Paragraph Formatting
8 Save a Document as a PDF

GO! Make It **Project 4A Part 2 Motion Testimony**

 PROJECT FILES

For Project 4A Client Mailing Part 2, you will need the following file:

w4A_Motion_Testimony

You will save your documents as:

Lastname_Firstname_4A_Motion_Testimony
Lastname_Firstname_4A_Motion_Testimony_PDF

PROJECT RESULTS

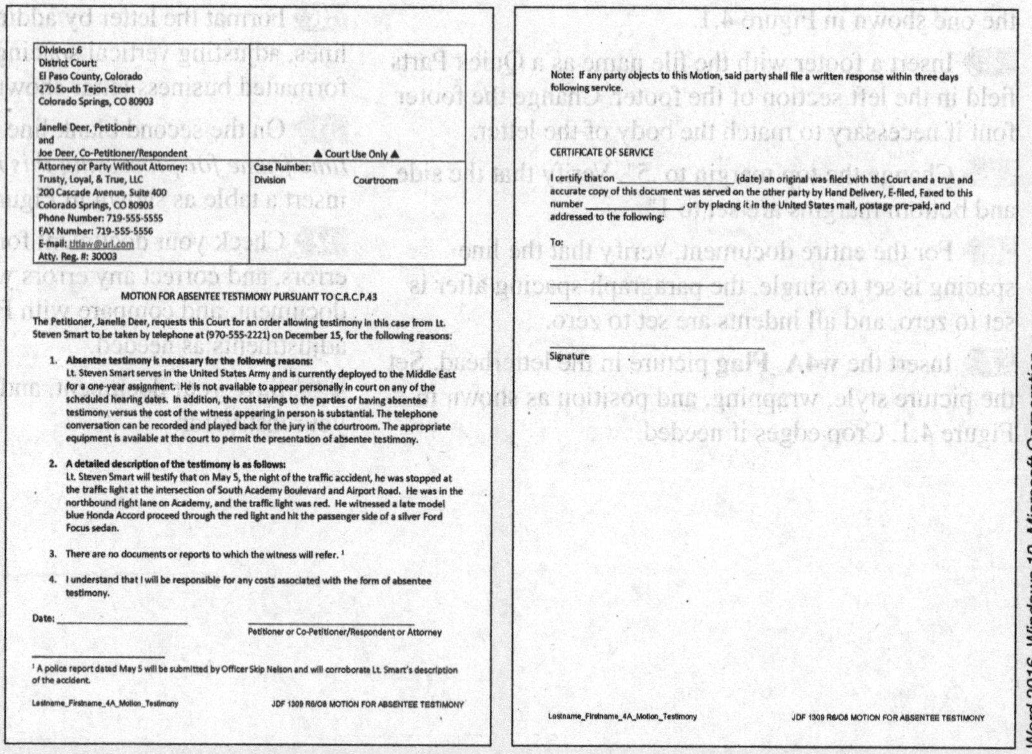

FIGURE 4.2 Project 4A, Part 2 Motion Testimony

Word 2016, Windows 10, Microsoft Corporation.

(Project 4A Part 2 Motion Testimony continues on the next page)

Figure content:

Division: 6
District Court:
El Paso County, Colorado
270 South Tejon Street
Colorado Springs, CO 80903

Janelle Deer, Petitioner
and
Joe Deer, Co-Petitioner/Respondent
Attorney or Party Without Attorney:
Trusty, Loyal, & True, LLC
200 Cascade Avenue, Suite 400
Colorado Springs, CO 80903
Phone Number: 719-555-5555
FAX Number: 719-555-5556
E-mail: tltlaw@url.com
Atty. Reg. #: 30003

▲ Court Use Only ▲

Case Number:
Division   Courtroom

MOTION FOR ABSENTEE TESTIMONY PURSUANT TO C.R.C.P.43

The Petitioner, Janelle Deer, requests this Court for an order allowing testimony in this case from Lt. Steven Smart to be taken by telephone at (970-555-2221) on December 15, for the following reasons:

1. **Absentee testimony is necessary for the following reasons:**
Lt. Steven Smart serves in the United States Army and is currently deployed to the Middle East for a one-year assignment. He is not available to appear personally in court on any of the scheduled hearing dates. In addition, the cost savings to the parties of having absentee testimony versus the cost of the witness appearing in person is substantial. The telephone conversation can be recorded and played back for the jury in the courtroom. The appropriate equipment is available at the court to permit the presentation of absentee testimony.

2. **A detailed description of the testimony is as follows:**
Lt. Steven Smart will testify that on May 5, the night of the traffic accident, he was stopped at the traffic light at the intersection of South Academy Boulevard and Airport Road. He was in the northbound right lane on Academy, and the traffic light was red. He witnessed a late model blue Honda Accord proceed through the red light and hit the passenger side of a silver Ford Focus sedan.

3. There are no documents or reports to which the witness will refer. [1]

4. I understand that I will be responsible for any costs associated with the form of absentee testimony.

Date: _____

_____
Petitioner or Co-Petitioner/Respondent or Attorney

[1] A police report dated May 5 will be submitted by Officer Skip Nelson and will corroborate Lt. Smart's description of the accident.

Lastname_Firstname_4A_Motion_Testimony   JDF 1309 R6/08 MOTION FOR ABSENTEE TESTIMONY

Right figure:

Note: If any party objects to this Motion, said party shall file a written response within three days following service.

CERTIFICATE OF SERVICE

I certify that on _____ (date) an original was filed with the Court and a true and accurate copy of this document was served on the other party by Hand Delivery, E-filed, Faxed to this number _____, or by placing it in the United States mail, postage pre-paid, and addressed to the following:

To:

Signature _____

Lastname_Firstname_4A_Motion_Testimony   JDF 1309 R6/08 MOTION FOR ABSENTEE TESTIMONY

108 Legal | Chapter 4: DISCIPLINE SPECIFIC PROJECTS

1 From the student files that accompany this text, locate and open the file w4A_Motion_Testimony, and then save the file in your **Legal Client Mailing folder** as **Lastname_ Firstname_4A_Motion_Testimony**. This document was revised with the Track Changes feature turned on. This feature is often used in law firms where it is important to track and display proposed revisions to legal documents. The revisions in the document indicate inserted and deleted text. You will create the document shown in Figure 4.2.

2 Insert a footer with the file name as a Quick Parts field. In the right section of the footer, insert the text **JDF 1309 R6/08 MOTION FOR ABSENTEE TESTIMONY**.

3 Accept or reject the changes marked in this document using the Track Changes feature of Word. The Track Changes feature is found on the Review tab on the ribbon. Make sure the *Display for Review* box is set to **All Markup**, and click *Track Changes* off if it is turned on. Starting from the beginning of the document, accept and reject changes as follows so that your document matches Figure 4.2.

- Reject the deletion of the phone number *2221*.
- Reject the addition of the phone number *1222*.
- Accept adding the full words *United* and *States*.
- Accept adding the sentence *The appropriate equipment is available at the court to permit the presentation of absentee testimony.*
- Accept adding the words *South* and *northbound*.
- Reject deleting the word *blue* and *reject* adding the words *dark green*.
- Accept deleting *3* and adding *three*.
- Reject deleting *United States* and adding *US*. Click OK.

4 At the beginning of the document, insert a table with two columns and two rows.

5 In the first column, in the first row of the table, type the following text:

Division: 6
District Court:
El Paso County, Colorado
270 South Tejon Street
Colorado Springs, CO 80903
Janelle Deer, Petitioner
and
Joe Deer, Co-Petitioner/Respondent

6 In the first column, in the second row of the table, type the following text:

Attorney or Party Without Attorney:
Trusty, Loyal, & True, LLC
200 Cascade Avenue, Suite 400
Colorado Springs, CO 80903
Phone Number: 719-555-5555
FAX Number: 719-555-5556
E-mail: tltlaw@url.com
Atty. Reg. #: 30003

7 In the second column, in the first row of the table, type the text **Court Use Only**. Insert a triangle symbol ▲ from Wingdings 3 before and after this text. Align text in cell to match Figure 4.2.

8 In the second column, in the second row of the table, type the following text as shown in Figure 4.2. (*Hint:* Press Ctrl+Tab two times to position the text *Courtroom*.)

| Case Number: | |
| Division | Courtroom |

9 Format the text to match Figure 4.2.

10 Find all instances of the word *Stephen*, and replace it with **Steven**.

(Project 4A Part 2 Motion Testimony continues on the next page)

GO! Make It | **Project 4A Part 2 Motion Testimony** (continued)

11 Apply numbering, indents, and spacing to match Figure 4.2.

12 At the end of numbered paragraph 3, enter a footnote that reads **A police report dated May 5 will be submitted by Officer Skip Nelson and will corroborate Lt. Smart's description of the accident.**

13 Change the top margin to .7". Insert check box symbols under the signature line as shown in Figure 4.2.

14 If necessary, make other adjustments to margins, line and paragraph spacing, capitalization, or other formatting to best match Figure 4.2. Proofread the document for spelling and grammar errors.

15 Preview the document comparing with Figure 4.2 and correct any errors you find. Save the document.

16 Save the document again as a PDF file with the name **Lastname_Firstname_4A_Motion_Testimony_PDF**.

17 Submit file(s) as directed by your instructor.

(Project 4A Part 2 Motion Testimony continues on the next page)

CONTENT-BASED ASSESSMENTS

Apply skills from these objectives:

1 Create Mailing Labels Using Mail Merge
2 Format a Table
3 Change Document and Paragraph Layout
4 Preview and Print a Document

 PROJECT FILES

For Project 4A Legal Client Mailing Part 3, you will need the following files:

New blank Word document

w4A_Legal_Addresses

You will save your document as:

Lastname_Firstname_4A_Client_Labels

PROJECT RESULTS

Ms. Rebecca Patterson	Mr. Ernest Aguilar	Ms. Audra Blanch
4321 Cascade Avenue, Suite 200	50 South Nevada Avenue	9175 Main Street
Colorado Springs, CO 80903	Colorado Springs, CO 80903	Security, CO 80911
Dr. Natasha Montgomery	Dr. Louis Valdez	Ms. Jen Li Wang
75 Tejon Street	5040 Widefield Avenue	900 Hancock Boulevard
Colorado Springs, CO 80903	Security, CO 80911	Colorado Springs, CO 80909
Ms. Warren Turner-Richardson	Ms. LaKeisha Washington	Dr. Adam Meiklejohn
100 Pikes Peak Avenue	39875 Blaney Road	222 East Airport Road
Colorado Springs, CO 80903	Fountain, CO 80817	Colorado Springs, CO 80909
Dr. Carter Smith		
87654 Santa Fe Drive		
Fountain, CO 80817		

Lastname_Firstname_4A_Client_Labels

Word 2016, Windows 10, Microsoft Corporation.

FIGURE 4.3 Project 4A, Part 3 Client Labels

(Project 4A Part 3 Client Labels continues on the next page)

CONTENT-BASED ASSESSMENTS

1 From the student files that accompany this text, locate and copy the file **w4A_Legal_Addresses** to your **Legal Client Mailing** folder.

2 Starting with a new blank Word document, use mail merge to create a labels document that looks like the client mailing labels shown in Figure 4.3. Your labels are Avery US Letter, 5160 Easy Peel Address labels, which measure 1" tall by 2.63" wide.

3 The recipient data source is **w4A_Legal_Addresses**.

4 Ensure that all lines fit in the label area. To avoid confusing this file with the end results file, save this file as **Lastname_Firstname_4A_Client_Label_Main** in your **Legal Client Mailing** folder.

5 Preview the document, and compare with Figure 4.3, making adjustments as needed. Save the main document.

6 At the end of the merge, *Edit individual labels* to create a new file with only the label text. Save your new address labels document in your **Legal Client Mailing** folder as **Lastname_Firstname_4A_Client_Labels**.

7 To the footer, add the file name as a Quick Parts field. If necessary, delete blank lines or row(s) at the bottom of the table so that the entire document fits on one page (even the blank labels). Modify the bottom margin if necessary to ensure the footer will appear on the page if printed. Save this as the end results file.

8 Submit file(s) as directed by your instructor.

CONTENT-BASED ASSESSMENTS

 GO! Make It   Project 4A Part 4 Client Form Letters

Apply skills from these objectives:

1 Create a New Document from an Existing Document

2 Merge a Data Source and a Main Document

3 Preview and Print a Document

📁 **PROJECT FILES**

For Project 4A Legal Client Mailing Part 4, you will need the following files:

w4A_Legal_Addresses

Lastname_Firstname_4A_Client_Letter (from Part 1 of this project)

You will save your document as:

Lastname_Firstname_4A_Client_Form_Letters

PROJECT RESULTS

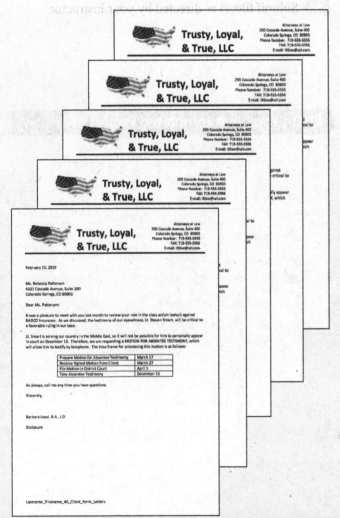

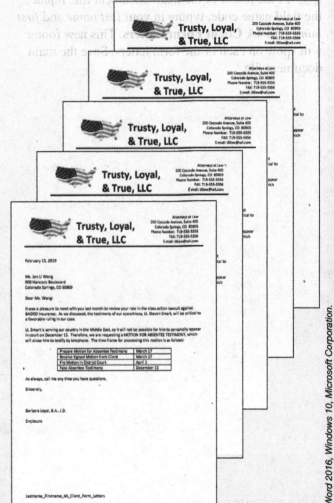

FIGURE 4.4 Project 4A, Part 4 Client Form Letters

(Project 4A Part 4 Client Form Letters continues on the next page)

CONTENT-BASED ASSESSMENTS

1 From your **Legal Client Mailing** folder, locate and open your file **Lastname_Firstname_4A_Client_Letter**. Save the file as **Lastname_Firstname_4A_Client_Main_Letter** so that you will not confuse it with your end results file. You will use mail merge to create a new document containing 12 form letters that look like the one shown in Figure 4.4.

2 The data source is **w4A_Legal_Addresses**. Insert a proper business letter address block and greeting line to match the content and punctuation in Figure 4.4.

3 In the footer of the main document file, replace the field name code, typing in your *last name* and *first name* and **4A Client Form Letters**. This new footer will show on each of the form letters. Save the main document file.

4 Preview the document and compare with Figure 4.4. Verify that the letters are properly formatted in the merge preview, and go back to fix as needed. Save the main document.

5 At the end of the merge, choose to *Edit individual letters* to create a new file with the 10 letters, one on each page. Save the file with the 10 letters as **Lastname_Firstname_4A_Client_Form_Letters** in the **Legal Client Mailing** folder. Save this as the end results file.

6 Submit file(s) as directed by your instructor.

> **END | You have completed Project 4A**

OUTCOMES-BASED ASSESSMENTS

Apply skills from these objectives:

1 Create a New Document from an Existing Document

2 Insert and Format Graphics

3 Change Document and Paragraph Layout

4 Change and Modify Lists

5 Use Special Character and Paragraph Formatting

GO! Think Project 4B Legal Stock Mailing: Part 1 Stock Letter

 PROJECT FILES

For Project 4B Legal Stock Mailing Part 1, you will need the following files:

w4B_Stock_Letter

w4B_Flag

You will save your document as:

Lastname_Firstname_4B_Stock_Letter

You are the assistant to the chief executive officer of Trusty, Loyal, & True, LLC, Attorneys at Law. Your office needs to prepare a letter to investors to accompany documents related to the purchase of preferred stock. Edit and properly format a one-page letter to accompany stock documents.

1 Create a folder in which to save your files for this project called **Legal Stock Mailing**. From the student files that accompany this text, locate and open the file **w4B_Stock_Letter**, and then save the file in your **Legal Stock Mailing** folder as **Lastname_Firstname_4B_Stock_Letter**.

2 Add the file name to the footer as a Quick Parts field.

3 Create a letterhead or reuse the one created in the prior project. Include the **w4B_Flag** logo graphic and a border.

4 Change line spacing, paragraph spacing, blank lines, and text in the letter as appropriate for a properly formatted one-page business letter.

5 Address the letter to:

Ms.	Jenny	Jager	1050 Garden of the Gods Road	Colorado Springs	CO	80907

6 Bullet the three documents listed.

7 Add an appropriate sentence or paragraph to the letter explaining that you are enclosing a paper about digital copyright law. You are doing this because some stockholders have asked questions about the company's involvement in web publishing.

8 Preview the document, and go back to adjust as needed. Adjust margins and font size appropriately to make the letter fit neatly on one page. Check the letter, and correct any spelling or grammar errors you find. Reference the example of a properly formatted business letter in the previous projector see proper business letter requirements in Appendix A.

9 Save the document and submit the letter file as directed by your instructor.

(Project 4B Part 2 Copyright Law Paper continues on the next page)

OUTCOMES-BASED ASSESSMENTS

Apply skills from these objectives:

1 Create a New Document from an Existing Document

2 Use Special Character and Paragraph Formatting

3 Change Document and Paragraph Layout

4 Create Citations and a Bibliography in a Research Paper

5 Insert Footnotes in a Research Paper

6 Change and Reorganize Text

7 Use Proofing Options

8 Preview and Print a Document

9 Save a Document as a PDF

 PROJECT FILES

For Project 4B Legal Stock Mailing Part 2, you will need the following file:

w4B_Copyright_Law

You will save your document as:

Lastname_Firstname_4B_Copyright_Law

You are a student in Professor Henry Kim's Business Law course. You have been asked to prepare a research paper about digital copyright using MLA 8th Edition format. Professor Kim is working with the lawyers at Trusty, Loyal, & True, LLC. The attorneys at Trusty, Loyal, & True, LLC will be distributing the best digital copyright paper from Professor Kim's class to investors in All About Stock Company.

1 From the student files that accompany this text, locate and open **w4B_Copyright_Law** and save it in your **Legal Stock Mailing** folder as **Lastname_Firstname_4B_Copyright_Law**.

2 Add the file name to the footer as a Quick Parts field.

3 Using MLA 8th Edition format, set the line and paragraph spacing and enter the first-page information. See Appendix B.

4 Format the page numbering and paragraph indents using MLA format.

5 On the second page, enter a footnote at the end of the first bullet: *Jeopardizing "fair use."* Enter the text of the note: **See TLT LLC internal memorandum** The Changing Face of Fair Use.

6 Enter three MLA 8th Edition sources using the Source Manager as follows:

- The first source, http://www.gseis.ucla.edu/iclp/dmca1.htm, has no named author, so use **UCLA Online Institute for Cyberspace Law and Policy** as the corporate author. Enter the title of the webpage: **The Digital Millennium Copyright Act**. Enter the date of publication, **2001 February 8**. For the date accessed, use the current date. For medium use the web address.

- The second source, http://www.eff.org/IP/DMCA/?f=unintended_consequences.html, has no named author, so use **Electronic Frontier Foundation** as the corporate author. Enter the title of the webpage: **Unintended Consequences: Seven Years under the DMCA**. Enter the date of publication, **2006 April 13**. For the date accessed, use the current date. For medium use the web address.

- The third source is a book titled **Patent, Copyright & Trademark: An Intellectual Property Desk Reference, 8th Edition**. The author is **Stim, Richard W**. It was published in **2006** in **Berkeley, CA**, by **NOLO**.

(Project 4B Part 2 Copyright Law Paper continues on the next page)

OUTCOMES-BASED ASSESSMENTS

7 Insert three MLA 8th Edition citations as follows:

- Near the end of the first paragraph after *According to the UCLA Online Institute for Cyberspace Law and Policy* and before the comma, enter a citation for **UCLA Online Institute for Cyberspace Law and Policy**.

- On the second page, in the paragraph starting *This federal statue*, at the end of the first sentence, right after *materials protected by copyright*, enter a citation for **Stim**. Edit to include page **227** in the citation.

- On the second page, at the end of the paragraph starting *This federal statue*, right after *unintended consequences* and before the comma, enter a citation for **Electronic Frontier Foundation**.

8 Create a reference page using the MLA 8th Edition format.

9 Preview, proof, and correct as needed. Save the document.

10 Save the document again as a PDF file.

11 Submit file(s) as directed by your instructor.

OUTCOMES-BASED ASSESSMENTS

Apply skills from these objectives:

1 Create Mailing Labels Using Mail Merge

2 Format a Table

3 Change Document and Paragraph Layout

4 Preview and Print a Document

GO! Think   Project 4B Part 3 Stock Labels

 PROJECT FILES

For Project 4B Legal Stock Mailing Part 3, you will need the following files:

New blank Word document

w4B_Stock_Addresses

You will save your document as:

Lastname_Firstname_4B_Stock_Labels

1 From the student files that accompany this text, locate and copy the file **w4B_Stock_Addresses** to your **Legal Stock Mailing** folder.

2 Start with a new blank Word document. To prevent confusion with the end results file, save the file as **Lastname_Firstname_4B_Stock_Labels_Main** in your **Legal Stock Mailing** folder.

3 Use mail merge to create labels. Your labels are Avery US Letter, 5160 Easy Peel Address labels, 1" tall by 2.63" wide.

4 Your recipient data source is the student data file **w4B_Stock_Addresses**.

5 Arrange your labels, and change spacing to ensure that all lines fit in the label area. Save the main document file.

6 After the merge is completed, *Edit individual labels* to create a new file with the labels. Save the document as **Lastname_Firstname_4B_Stock_Labels**.

7 To the footer, add the file name as a Quick Parts field. If necessary, delete blank lines or row(s) at the bottom of the table so that the entire document fits on one page (even the blank labels). Modify the bottom margin if necessary to ensure the footer will appear on the page if printed. Save this as the end results file.

8 Submit file(s) as directed by your instructor.

OUTCOMES-BASED ASSESSMENTS

GO! Think Project 4B Part 4 Stock Form Letters

Apply skills from these objectives:

1 Create a New Document from an Existing Document

2 Merge a Data Source and a Main Document

3 Preview and Print a Document

 PROJECT FILES

For Project 4B Legal Stock Mailing Part 4, you will need the following files:

Lastname_Firstname_4B_Stock_Letter (from Part 1 of this project)
w4B_Stock_Addresses

You will save your document as:

Lastname_Firstname_4B_Stock_Form_Letters

1 From your **Legal Stock Mailing** folder, locate and open your file **Lastname_Firstname_4B_Stock_Letter**. Save the file as **Lastname_Firstname_4B_Stock_Main_Lette**r to prevent confusion with your end results file. Use mail merge to create properly formatted business letters.

2 In the footer of the main letter file, replace the field name code, typing in your *last name* and *first name* and **4B Stock Form Letters**. This new footer will show on each of the form letters.

3 Use mail merge to create properly formatted business letters to each person in the data source. The data source is the student data file **w4B_Stock_Addresses**. Preview the document, and go back to adjust as needed. Save the main document file.

4 After the merge is completed, *Edit individual letters* to create a new file with all the form letters with proper business letter format.

5 Save this end results file as **Lastname_Firstname_4B_Stock_Form_Letters**.

6 Submit file(s) as directed by your instructor.

END | You have completed Project 4B

Project 4C Stockholder Ledger

 PROJECT FILES

For Project 4C, you will need the following file:

e4C_Stockholder_Ledger

You will save your workbook as:

Lastname_Firstname_4C_Stockholder_Ledger

Apply skills from these objectives:

1 Enter Data in a Worksheet

2 Construct and Copy Formulas and Use the SUM Function

3 Construct Formulas for Mathematical Operations

4 Format Cells with Merge & Center and Cell Styles

5 Check Spelling in a Worksheet

6 Format a Worksheet

7 Navigate a Workbook and Rename Worksheets

8 Edit and Format Multiple Worksheets at the Same Time

9 Create a Summary Sheet

10 Sort Data

11 Chart Data to Create a Bar Chart

PROJECT RESULTS

Trusty, Loyal, & True, LLC

THE HOYLE COMPANY
Stockholder Report

Stockholder	Common Shares	Percent of Total Common Stock	Preferred Shares	Percent of Total Preferred Stock	Total Common and Preferred Shares	Percent of Total Common and Preferred Stock
SureFire Investment Group	650,000	6.2%	143,000	7.0%	793,000	6.3%
Stability Holdings, Inc.	45,000	0.4%	59,361	2.9%	104,361	0.8%
Warren and Company	39,611	0.4%	125,000	6.1%	164,611	1.3%
Rags to Riches Co.	874,362	8.4%	41,620	2.0%	915,982	7.3%
Rodie Resources	120,500	1.2%	25,000	1.2%	145,500	1.2%
Meiklejohn International Corporation	120,500	1.2%	87,652	4.3%	208,152	1.7%
Good, Better, and Best Investments	67,333	0.6%	35,859	1.8%	103,192	0.8%
Portfolio Plus	90,000	0.9%	70,000	3.4%	160,000	1.3%
Strategic Planning Group	-	0.0%	2,968	0.1%	2,968	0.0%
Triple Balances		0.0%	360,360	17.6%	360,360	2.9%
Hoyle Enterprises	4,500,000	43.0%	345,500	16.9%	4,845,500	38.8%
RichDad Bank of America	-	0.0%	448,752	21.9%	448,752	3.6%
Blanch and Associates	1,200,000	11.5%	27,664	1.4%	1,227,664	9.8%
Worldwide Investments, Inc.	150,000	1.4%	-	0.0%	150,000	1.2%
Jardine Financial Management Corp.	750,000	7.2%	9,221	0.5%	759,221	6.1%
Fortune 1000 Company	-	0.0%	91,525	4.5%	91,525	0.7%
Marshall & Howard	100,000	1.0%		0.0%	100,000	0.8%
Bright Future Ahead Co.	250,000	2.4%		0.0%	250,000	2.0%
Mendenhall Millionaires Club	750,000	7.2%	17,670	0.9%	767,670	6.1%
Sopko Securities, Inc.	750,000	7.2%	153,426	7.5%	903,426	7.2%
TOTAL STOCK	**10,457,306**		**2,044,578**		**12,501,884**	

Lastname_Firstname_4C_Stockholder_Ledger

Stockholder Report

Excel 2016, Windows 10, Microsoft Corporation.

FIGURE 4.5 Project 4C Stockholder Ledger

(Project 4C Stockholder Ledger continues on the next page)

CONTENT-BASED ASSESSMENTS

1 Create a folder in which to store your files for this project called **Stockholder Ledger**.

2 From the student files that accompany this text, locate and open the file **e4C_Stockholder_Ledger**, and then save the file in your **Stockholder Ledger** folder as **Lastname_Firstname_4C_Stockholder_Ledger**. You will modify the workbook to match the worksheets shown in Figures 4.5, 4.6, and 4.7.

3 Group the two worksheets, and then modify both simultaneously as follows:

- In the left section of the header, insert the text *Trusty, Loyal, && True, LLC. (Type both ampersands; only one will show in the header.)*
- Insert the file name code and the sheet name code in the footer.
- Change the page orientation to Landscape.
- Ungroup the sheets.

4 Modify Sheet1 only, as follows:

- Verify that the sheets are ungrouped. Select Sheet1.
- Rename Sheet1 **Stockholder Report**.
- Set the worksheet so it will be centered horizontally on the printed page.
- Set column titles to match the Figure 4.5, using bold, alignment, text wrapping, column width, and row height.
- Format title to match Figure 4.5.
- Enter and fill formulas to total the number of common and preferred shares for each stockholder.
- Use SUM functions to total each of the three columns: Common Shares, Preferred Shares, and Total Common and Preferred Shares.
- Enter and fill formulas, with absolute cell referencing, to calculate for each stockholder their percent of total common stock based on the total of the common shares.
- Enter and fill formulas, with absolute cell referencing, to calculate for each stockholder their percent of preferred stock.
- Enter and fill formulas, with absolute cell referencing, to calculate for each stockholder their percent of total common and preferred stock.
- Apply cell styles, align and format numbers, apply fill color, and apply borders as shown in Figure 4.5.

(Project 4C Stockholder Ledger continues on the next page)

Trusty, Loyal, & True, LLC

THE HOYLE COMPANY
Stockholder Report - Proxy/Voting for Annual Meeting

Stockholder	Percent of Common Stock	Percent of Preferred Stock	Percent of Total Common and Preferred Stock	Proxy Received
SureFire Investment Group	6.2%	7.0%	6.3%	✓
Warren and Company	0.4%	6.1%	1.3%	✓
Rags to Riches Co.	8.4%	2.0%	7.3%	✓
Rodie Resources	1.2%	1.2%	1.2%	✓
Meiklejohn International Corporation	1.2%	4.3%	1.7%	✓
Strategic Planning Group	0.0%	0.1%	0.0%	
Blanch and Associates	11.5%	1.4%	9.8%	✓
Jardine Financial Management Corp.	7.2%	0.5%	6.1%	✓
Marshall & Howard	1.0%	0.0%	0.8%	✓
Mendenhall Millionaires Club	7.2%	0.9%	6.1%	✓
Sopko Securities, Inc.	7.2%	7.5%	7.2%	✓
Good, Better, and Best Investments	0.6%	1.8%	0.8%	✓
Stability Holdings, Inc.	0.4%	2.9%	0.8%	
Portfolio Plus	0.9%	3.4%	1.3%	
Triple Balances	0.0%	17.6%	2.9%	
Hoyle Enterprises	43.0%	16.9%	38.8%	
RichDad Bank of America	0.0%	21.9%	3.6%	
Worldwide Investments, Inc.	1.4%	0.0%	1.2%	
Fortune 1000 Company	0.0%	4.5%	0.7%	
Bright Future Ahead Co.	2.4%	0.0%	2.0%	
TOTAL STOCK	**100.0%**	**100.0%**	**100.0%**	

Need two thirds or 67% for an official

PERCENT OF COMMON STOCK REPRESENTED BY PROXY	51.9%
PERCENT OF PREFERRED STOCK REPRESENTED BY PROXY	32.7%

Lastname_Firstname_4C_Stockholder_Ledger

Proxy Tabulation

Excel 2016, Windows 10, Microsoft Corporation.

FIGURE 4.6 Project 4C Stockholder Ledger

5 Modify Sheet2 only, as follows:

- Rename Sheet2 **Proxy Tabulation**.

- Set the worksheet so it will be centered horizontally on the printed page.

- Format title to match Figure 4.6.

- Set column titles to match Figure 4.6, using bold, alignment, text wrapping, column width, and row height.

- In the Percent of Common Stock column, enter and fill a formula referencing a cell on the Stockholder Report worksheet. Do the same to reference Percent of Preferred Stock and Percent of Total Common and Preferred Stock.

- Total the percentages in each column to verify a total of 100%.

- Insert a check mark symbol, Wingdings character 252, in the Proxy Received column for cells E4, E6, E7, E8, E9, E10, E12, E16, E18, E20, E22, and E23, as in Figure 4.6.

- Select a range including all the stockholder's names, their percentages, and the check marks. Sort by the Proxy Received column with the check marks.

- Enter a formula to total the percent of common stock represented by proxy. (Hint: Add the percentages of common stock for the companies marked with a check mark.)

(Project 4C Stockholder Ledger continues on the next page)

- Enter a formula to total the percent of preferred stock represented by proxy. (Hint: Add the percentages of preferred stock for the companies marked with a check mark.)
- Format to match Figure 4.6, apply row height, column width, fill color, borders, and bold as shown in Figure 4.6.
- As shown in Figure 4.6, insert a text box with the text **Need two-thirds or 67% for an official vote**.

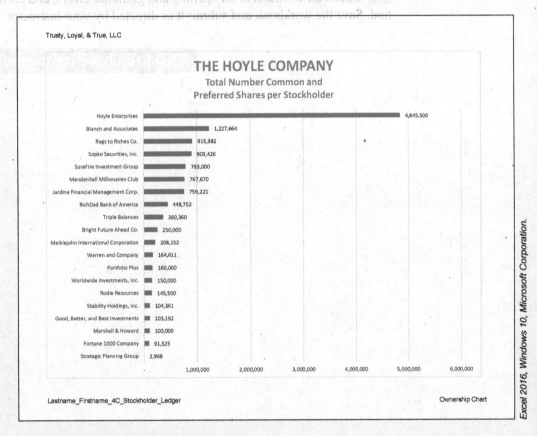

Trusty, Loyal, & True, LLC

THE HOYLE COMPANY
Total Number Common and
Preferred Shares per Stockholder

Stockholder	Shares
Hoyle Enterprises	4,845,500
Blanch and Associates	1,227,664
Rags to Riches Co.	915,982
Sopko Securities, Inc.	903,426
SureFire Investment Group	793,000
Mendenhall Millionaires Club	767,670
Jardine Financial Management Corp.	759,221
RichDad Bank of America	448,752
Triple Balances	360,360
Bright Future Ahead Co.	250,000
Meiklejohn International Corporation	208,152
Warren and Company	164,611
Portfolio Plus	160,000
Worldwide Investments, Inc.	150,000
Rodie Resources	145,500
Stability Holdings, Inc.	104,361
Good, Better, and Best Investments	103,192
Marshall & Howard	100,000
Fortune 1000 Company	91,525
Strategic Planning Group	2,968

Lastname_Firstname_4C_Stockholder_Ledger   Ownership Chart

Excel 2016, Windows 10, Microsoft Corporation.

FIGURE 4.7 Project 4C Stockholder Ledger

6 Create a bar chart as follows:

- Insert a new worksheet at the far right on which to arrange the chart data. Name the sheet tab **Chart Data**.
- Insert the file name code and the sheet name code in the footer.
- In the left section of the header, insert the text *Trusty, Loyal, && True, LLC*. (Type two ampersands; only one will show in the header.)
- Return to the Stockholder Report worksheet. Copy all the shareholder names and the number of common and preferred shares for each shareholder to the new sheet.
- Sort by the column with the number of common and preferred shares, smallest to largest.
- Use this data to create a bar chart as shown in Figure 4.7. Move the chart to a new sheet named **Ownership Chart**.

(Project 4C Stockholder Ledger continues on the next page)

- Format the chart title, layout, and style as shown in Figure 4.7.
- Insert the file name code and the sheet name code in the chart sheet footer.
- In the left section of the chart sheet header, insert the text *Trusty, Loyal, && True, LLC.* (Type two ampersands; only one will show in the header.)
- Move the Ownership Chart worksheet to the right of the Proxy Tabulation sheet.

7 Check all worksheets for spelling and grammar errors, and correct any errors you find. Save the workbook and submit it as directed by your instructor.

END | You have completed Project 4C

OUTCOMES-BASED ASSESSMENTS

GO! Think   Project 4D Billable Hours

Apply skills from these objectives:

1 Enter Data in a Worksheet

2 Construct and Copy Formulas and Use the SUM Function

3 Format Cells with Merge & Center and Cell Styles

4 Check Spelling in a Worksheet

5 Construct Formulas for Mathematical Operations

6 Edit Values in a Worksheet

7 Format a Worksheet

8 Navigate a Workbook and Rename Worksheets

9 Edit and Format Multiple Worksheets at the Same Time

10 Create a Summary Sheet

11 Chart Data with a Pie Chart

12 Format a Pie Chart

 PROJECT FILES

For Project 4D, you will need the following file:

e4D_Billable_Hours

You will save your workbook as:

Lastname_Firstname_4D_Billable_Hours

One of your new duties at the law firm of Trusty, Loyal, & True, LLC is to maintain a record of billable hours for specific cases. You have been provided with a workbook that contains a rough design along with the estimated billable hours for a case. You need to compute estimated total hours, actual total hours, and estimated and actual fees. You will also need to create worksheets to track actual hours and a chart showing the breakdown of each employee's percentage of the fees for the case.

1 Create a folder in which to store your files for this project called **Billable Hours**.

2 From the student files that accompany this text, locate and open the file **e4D_Billable_Hours**, and then save it to your **Billable Hours** folder as **Lastname_Firstname_4D_Billable_Hours**. Modify the existing Firm Billable Hours worksheet as follows:

- Change the orientation to Landscape.
- In the footer, insert the file name and sheet name codes.
- To the right of the estimated hours for each employee, insert a new blank column to record the actual hours of work. For each of the employees, enter the text **Actual Hours** as a column heading title.
- Format the Title and column headings. Use merge and center, text wrapping, cell styles, bold, alignment, borders, row height, and column width as needed.
- Use the following hourly rates:

Employee	Hourly Rate
Karen Garcia	$300
Rob Li	$200
Karla Hoyle	$80

- Total the estimated billable hours for each person.
- Enter formulas for each employee to calculate the total estimated hourly fees based on the hourly rate and total billable hours.
- Although there are no actual hours in the worksheet yet, enter formulas to total the actual hours and calculate actual hourly fees.
- Format the worksheet professionally. If necessary, adjust the margins and column widths so that the worksheet fits on one page.

(Project 4D Billable Hours continues on the next page)

OUTCOMES-BASED ASSESSMENTS

3 Create worksheets to track actual hours on each task as follows. Insert a new blank worksheet; name the sheet tab **Legal Assistant Actual Hours**. Copy the tasks from the Firm Billable Hours worksheet to a column in this worksheet. To the right, type column headings **Date** and **# of Hours**. These columns will be used to record actual dates and hours worked on each task.

4 Copy this worksheet to create two new worksheets for recording actual dates and hours for the partner and the associate. Name the worksheets **Partner Actual Hours** and **Associate Actual Hours**.

5 On each of the three actual hours worksheets, enter hypothetical dates and numbers of hours. Insert additional rows or columns to record additional dates and hours worked.

6 Group the worksheets and total the hypothetical actual number of hours worked on each task by each employee. In the footer, insert the file name and sheet name codes. Format neatly and professionally. Ungroup when done.

7 Return to the Firm Billable Hours worksheet. On the Firm Billable Hours worksheet, replace the prior formulas for total actual billable hours with formulas referencing the Actual Hours cells from the three actual hours worksheets.

8 Insert a text box and arrow calling attention to the difference between estimated hours and actual hours for one of the employees.

9 Create a pie chart to show each employee's percentage breakdown of the total actual hourly fees. Move the chart to a new worksheet, and then name the chart as **Fees Breakdown Chart**.

10 Check all worksheets for spelling and grammar errors. Save the workbook and submit it as directed by your instructor.

END | You have completed Project 4D

CONTENT-BASED ASSESSMENTS

PROJECT FILES

For Project 4E, you will need the following files:

New blank Access database
a4E_Caseload.xlsx (Excel file)

You will save your database as:

Lastname_Firstname_4E_Caseload.accdb

PROJECT RESULTS

Apply skills from these objectives:

1 Create a Table and Define Fields in a Blank Desktop Database
2 Change the Structure of Tables and Add a Second Table
3 Create and Use a Form to Add and Delete Records
4 Create Table Relationships
5 Create a Query in Query Design
6 Sort Query Results
7 Specify Criteria in a Query
8 Specify Numeric Criteria in a Query
9 Use Compound Criteria in a Query
10 Use Wildcards in a Query
11 Create Calculated Fields in a Query
12 Create a Query Based on More Than One Table
13 Create a Report Using the Report Wizard
14 Modify the Design of a Report
15 Close a Database and Exit Access

Lastname_Firstname_4E_Staff   8/24/2019

Staff ID	Last Name	First Name	Specialty	Billing Rate	CP, RP, PP	Hire Date
TLT1	Blanch	Carlos	Real Estate	$120.00	☑	5/1/1996
TLT2	Talladega	William	Estate and Trusts	$120.00	☑	5/1/2006
TLT3	Rodriguez	Alexander	Family Law	$100.00	☑	8/25/2011
TLT4	Johnson	Penny	Family Law	$90.00	☐	7/15/2012
TLT5	Loyal	Jennifer	Personal Injury	$90.00	☑	1/2/2013
TLT6	Reynolds	Adam	Real Estate	$80.00	☑	2/15/2016
TLT7	Garica	Karen	Litigation	$80.00	☑	2/15/2016
TLT8	Li	Rob	Litigation	$75.00	☐	8/1/2016
TLT9	Tanaka	Hanne	Workers' Compens	$75.00	☐	8/1/2016

Page 1

FIGURE 4.8 Project 4E Caseload Database—Staff Table

(Project 4E Caseload Database continues on the next page)

1 > Create a new folder in which to store your files for this project named **Caseload Database**.

2 > From the student data files that accompany this text, locate and copy the Excel file **a4E_Caseload** to your **Caseload Database** folder.

3 > Create a new blank desktop database, saving it in your **Caseload Database** folder. Name the database **Lastname_Firstname_4E_Caseload**.

4 > Create a table as shown in Figure 4.8 to store general information about the staff employed by the firm. Create the following fields, and name the table **Lastname_Firstname_4E_Staff**.

Field Name	Data Type	Description
ID	AutoNumber	
Last Name	Short Text	
First Name	Short Text	
Specialty	Short Text	Primary area of expertise
Billing Rate	Currency	Rate set by managing partners
CP, RP, PP	Yes/No	Check if Certified, Registered, or Professional
Hire Date	Date/Time	

5 > Change the table structure as shown in Figure 4.8 of **Lastname_Firstname_4E_Staff**.

- Rename the **ID** field **Staff ID**.
- Change the data type for **Staff ID** to *Short Text*.
- Set the **Staff ID** field as the primary key field.
- Change the *Field Size* property for **Staff ID** field to **5**.
- Set the *Format* property for **Billing Rate** to two decimal places. Save the changes.

6 > In Datasheet view, add records for the five staff members listed below as shown in Figure 4.8, and then save and close the table.

Staff ID	Last Name	First Name	Specialty	Billing Rate	CP, RP, PP	Hire Date
TLT1	Blanch	Carlos	Real Estate	$120.00	Yes	5/1/1996
TLT2	Talladega	William	Estate and Trusts	$120.00	Yes	5/1/2006
TLT3	Rodriguez	Alexander	Family Law	$100.00	Yes	8/25/2011
TLT4	Johnson	Penny	Family Law	$90.00	No	7/15/2012
TLT5	Loyal	Jennifer	Personal Injury	$90.00	Yes	1/2/2013

(Project 4E Caseload Database continues on the next page)

7 Create a form for this table, and accept the default name. Switch to Form view, and use the form to add the following data for four additional staff members as shown in Figure 4.8.

TLT6	TLT7
Reynolds, Adam	Garcia, Karen
Real Estate	Litigation
$80.00	$80.00
Yes (Certified CP)	Yes (Certified RP)
2/15/2016	2/15/2016

TLT8	TLT9
Li, Rob	Tanaka, Hanne
Litigation	Workers' Compensation
$75.00	$75.00
Not certified	Not certified
4/15/2016	8/1/2016

8 Close all open objects.

9 Import the Excel workbook named **a4E_Caseload** into this database as shown in Figure 4.9. (The figure shows the table after import and the entry of two additional records in the next step of the project.)

- Use the first row as column headings.
- Select the option for no primary key.
- Ensure that the **Billable Hours** field has a *Number* data type.
- Name the table **Lastname_Firstname_4E_Caseload**.

10 Create a form for this new table, and save it with the default name. Use the form to add two more cases to the database.

Assign staff member Li, **TLT8**, to the following case:	Assign staff member Garcia, **TLT7**, to the following case:
Case Number: **WC6754**	Case Number: **BR8779**
Case Name: **Martinez vs. Bear Mountain Mining**	Case Name: **Sopko vs. National Savings & Loan**
Client Name: **Martinez, Carl**	Client Name: **Sopko, Kay**
Billable Hours: **0**	Billable Hours: **0**
Date Opened: **7/14/2019**	Date Opened: **7/15/2019**
Date Closed: (leave blank)	Date Closed: (leave blank)

(Project 4E Caseload Database continues on the next page)

PROJECT RESULTS

Lastname_Firstname_4E_Caseload							8/24/2019
Staff ID	**Case Number**	**Case Name**	**Client Last Name**	**Client First Name**	**Billable Hours**	**Date Opened**	**Date Closed**
TLT1	PI5509	Deer vs. JLK Insurance	Deer	Janelle	271	3/14/2019	9/25/2019
TLT1	PI5513	Liang vs. Asian Express Lunchbox	Liang	Shen	566	8/14/2019	12/22/2019
TLT1	PI5578	Gibson vs. Martin	Martin	Harvey	75	4/14/2019	5/31/2019
TLT2	ET8792	Wellington vs. Estate of Ronald Carter	Carter	Tiffany	126	5/1/2019	11/3/2019
TLT2	EL1346	O'Brien vs. RestEasy Nursing Home	O'Brien	Martha	111	9/4/2019	
TLT2	ET8107	Sanchez, Maria vs. Ortiz, Roberto	Ortiz	Roberto	78	1/30/2019	4/28/2019
TLT3	RL4417	American Goodbank vs. Montaque	Montaque	Ariel	94	6/18/2019	
TLT3	RL4009	Hoyle vs. Peakview Homeowners' Association	Hoyle	Nancy	197	2/20/2019	5/13/2019
TLT3	RL4329	Robinson vs. Praire Water District	Robinson	Devon	389	3/25/2019	8/27/2019
TLT4	FL3495	Sieger vs. Chang	Sieger	Constance	41	7/1/2019	
TLT4	FL3497	Alvarez, John vs. Alvarez, Christina	Alvarez	John	209	3/12/2019	10/31/2019
TLT4	FL3602	Mendenhall vs. Conrad	Mendenhall	Jean	44	6/28/2019	
TLT5	FL3498	Smith, Gloria vs. Smith, Roger	Smith	Gloria	196	1/27/2019	6/10/2019
TLT5	FL3497	Alvarez, John vs. Alvarez, Christina	Alvarez	John	351	3/12/2019	10/31/2019
TLT5	FL3602	Mendenhall vs. Conrad	Mendenhall	Jean	65	6/28/2019	9/16/2019
TLT6	EM1430	Stevenson vs. Allied Processing	Stevenson	Arnold	439	3/7/2019	9/14/2019
TLT7	RL4408	Foster vs. Family Go Karts	Foster	Martin	83	4/28/2019	8/12/2019
TLT7	RL4009	Hoyle vs. Peakview Homeowners' Association	Hoyle	Nancy	429	2/20/2019	5/9/2019
TLT7	BR8779	Sopko vs. National Savings & Loan	Sopko	Kay	0	7/15/2019	
TLT8	WC6782	Jardine vs. Monument Precision Cuts	Jardine	Renee	162	5/9/2019	
TLT8	WC5555	Bailey vs. Rocky Mountain Chemicals	Bailey	Susan	621	2/2/2019	6/18/2019
TLT8	WC6754	Martinez vs. Bear Mountain Mining	Martinez	Carl	0	7/14/2019	
TLT9	WC6749	Rhode vs. Front Range Manufacturing	Rhode	Karla	705	9/20/2019	7/1/2019
TLT9	PI5513	Liang vs. Asian Express Lunchbox	Liang	Shen	312	8/14/2019	12/22/2019
TLT9	WC5555	Bailey vs. Rocky Mountain Chemicals	Bailey	Susan	293	2/2/2019	6/18/2019

Page 1

Access 2016, Windows 10, Microsoft Corporation.

FIGURE 4.9 Project 4E Caseload Database—Caseload Table

11 Create a one-to-many relationship between the two tables.

- Use the **Staff ID** field.
- Enforce referential integrity. Save the relationship.
- Close the relationship window and any open objects.

(Project 4E Caseload Database continues on the next page)

PROJECT RESULTS

Lastname_Firstname_4E_Real_Estate_Specialty				8/24/2019
Staff ID	**Last Name**	**Specialty**	**Hire Date**	
TLT1	Blanch	Real Estate	5/1/1996	
TLT6	Reynolds	Real Estate	2/15/2016	

Page 1

Access 2016, Windows 10, Microsoft Corporation.

FIGURE 4.10 Project 4E Caseload Database—Real Estate Specialty Query

12 Create a query as shown in Figure 4.10, using the **Lastname_Firstname_4E_Staff** table.

- Use **Staff ID, Last Name, Specialty,** and **Hire Date**.
- Sort by **Hire Date** in ascending order.
- Set the criteria to display those with a *Real Estate* **Specialty**.
- Save the query as **Lastname_Firstname_4E_Real_Estate_Specialty**, and close the query.

(Project 4E Caseload Database continues on the next page)

PROJECT RESULTS

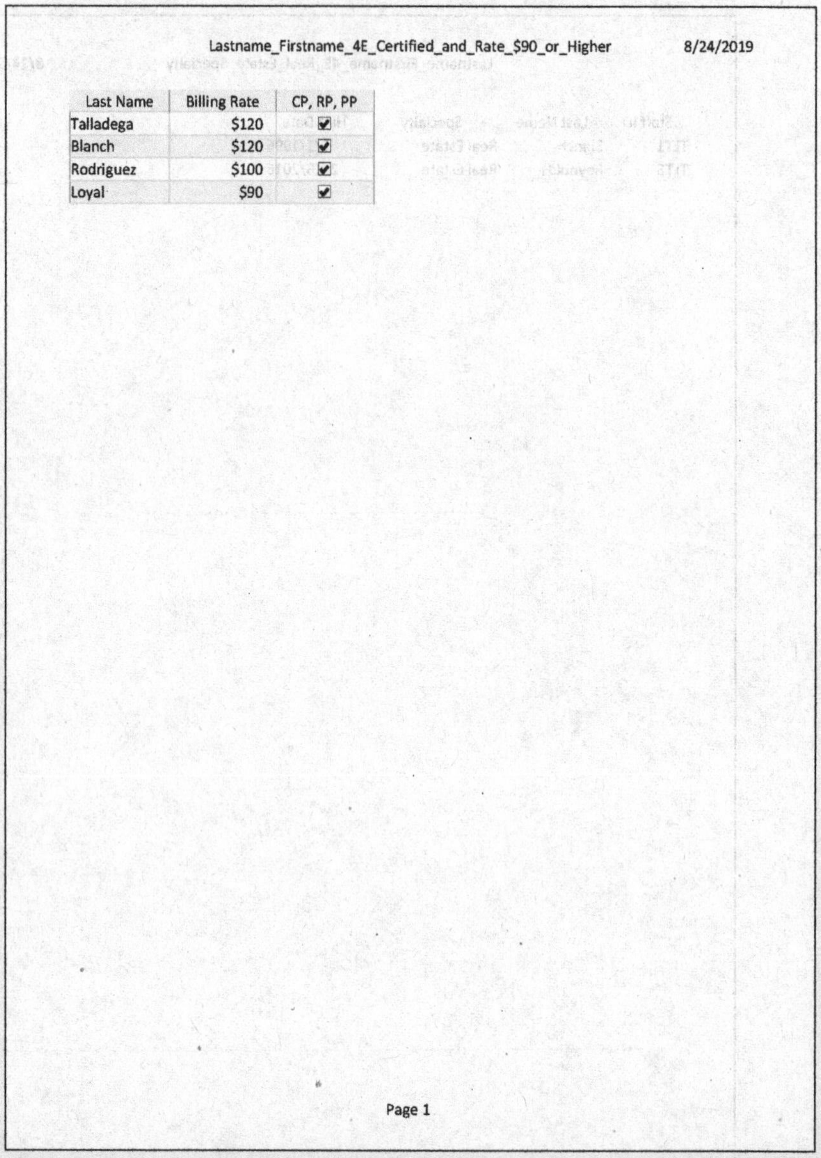 Lastname_Firstname_4E_Certified_and_Rate_$90_or_Higher			8/24/2019
Last Name	**Billing Rate**	**CP, RP, PP**	
Talladega	$120	☑	
Blanch	$120	☑	
Rodriguez	$100	☑	
Loyal	$90	☑	

Page 1

Access 2016, Windows 10, Microsoft Corporation.

FIGURE 4.11 Project 4E Caseload Database—Certified and Rate $90 or Higher Query

13 Create a query as shown in Figure 4.11, using **Lastname Firstname 4E Staff** table.

- Use **Last Name**, **Billing Rate**, and **CP, RP, PP.**

- Set the criteria to display those that have a **Billing Rate** of *$90 or higher* and the **CP, RP, PP** field indicating *yes*, they have a type of certification.

- Sort by **Billing Rate** in descending order.

- Set the properties for the **Billing Rate** field to zero decimal places.

- Save the query as **Lastname_Firstname_4E_Certified_and_Rate_$90_or_Higher**, and close the query.

(Project 4E Caseload Database continues on the next page)

PROJECT RESULTS

Lastname_Firstname_4E_Hired_2012-2016			8/24/2019
Last Name	**First Name**	**Specialty**	**Hire Date**
Johnson	Penny	Family Law	7/15/2012
Loyal	Jennifer	Personal Injury	1/2/2013
Garica	Karen	Litigation	2/15/2016
Reynolds	Adam	Real Estate	2/15/2016
Tanaka	Hanne	Workers' Compens	8/1/2016
Li	Rob	Litigation	8/1/2016

Page 1

Access 2016, Windows 10, Microsoft Corporation.

FIGURE 4.12 Project 4E Caseload Database—Hired 2012–2016 Query

14 ▶ Create a query as shown in Figure 4.12, using the **Lastname_Firstname_4E_Staff** table.

- Use **Last Name**, **First Name**, **Specialty**, and **Hire Date**.
- Set the criteria to display those that were hired BETWEEN 1/2/2012 AND 12/31/2016.
- Sort by **Hire Date** in ascending order.
- Save the query as **Lastname_Firstname_4E_Hired_2012-2016**, and close the query.

(Project 4E Caseload Database continues on the next page)

PROJECT RESULTS

Staff ID	Case Number	Case Name	Date Opened	Date Closed
		Lastname_Firstname_4E_Estate_Trust_and_Elder_Law_Cases		8/24/2019
TLT2	ET8107	Sanchez, Maria vs. Ortiz, Roberto	1/30/2019	4/28/2019
TLT6	EM1430	Stevenson vs. Allied Processing	3/7/2019	9/14/2019
TLT2	ET8792	Wellington vs. Estate of Ronald Carter	5/1/2019	11/3/2019
TLT2	EL1346	O'Brien vs. RestEasy Nursing Home	9/4/2019	

Page 1

Access 2016, Windows 10, Microsoft Corporation.

FIGURE 4.13 Project 4E Caseload Database—Estate Trust and Elder Law Cases Query

15 Create a query as shown in Figure 4.13, using the
Lastname_Firstname_4E_Caseload table.

- Use **Staff ID**, **Case Number**, **Case Name**, **Date Opened**, and **Date Closed**.
- Enter criteria using a wildcard in the **Case Number** field to display only estate trust and elder law cases, which will have **Case Numbers** that begin with the letter **E**.
- Sort by **Date Opened** in ascending order.
- Save the query as **Lastname_Firstname_4E_Estate_Trust_and_Elder_Law_Cases**, and close the query.

(Project 4E Caseload Database continues on the next page)

PROJECT RESULTS

Case Number	Case Name	Client Last Name	Date Opened
	Lastname_Firstname_4E_Open_Cases		8/24/2019
WC6782	Jardine vs. Monument Precision Cuts	Jardine	5/9/2019
RL4417	American Goodbank vs. Montaque	Montaque	6/18/2019
FL3602	Mendenhall vs. Conrad	Mendenhall	6/28/2019
FL3495	Sieger vs. Chang	Sieger	7/1/2019
WC6754	Martinez vs. Bear Mountain Mining	Martinez	7/14/2019
BR8779	Sopko vs. National Savings & Loan	Sopko	7/15/2019
EL1346	O'Brien vs. RestEasy Nursing Home	O'Brien	9/4/2019

Page 1

FIGURE 4.14 Project 4E Caseload Database—Open Cases Query

Access 2016, Windows 10, Microsoft Corporation.

16 Create a query as shown in Figure 4.14, using the **Lastname_Firstname_4E_Caseload** table.

- Use **Case Number**, **Case Name**, **Client Last Name**, **Date Opened**, and **Date Closed**.

- Use the *Is Null* criteria to display the cases that do not have a **Date Closed** date.

- Sort by the **Date Opened** field in ascending order.

- Clear the Show check box for the **Date Closed** field.

- Save the query as **Lastname_Firstname_4E_Open_Cases**, and close the query.

(Project 4E Caseload Database continues on the next page)

PROJECT RESULTS

Staff ID	Last Name	First Name	Case Number	Billable Hours	Caseload Fees
			Lastname_Firstname_4E_Total_Caseload_Fees		8/16/2019
TLT1	Blanch	Carlos	PI5513	566	$67,920
TLT1	Blanch	Carlos	PI5578	75	$9,000
TLT1	Blanch	Carlos	PI5509	271	$32,520
TLT2	Talladega	William	ET8792	126	$15,120
TLT2	Talladega	William	EL1346	111	$13,320
TLT2	Talladega	William	ET8107	78	$9,360
TLT3	Rodriguez	Alexander	RL4417	94	$9,400
TLT3	Rodriguez	Alexander	RL4009	197	$19,700
TLT3	Rodriguez	Alexander	RL4329	389	$38,900
TLT4	Johnson	Penny	FL3602	44	$3,960
TLT4	Johnson	Penny	FL3495	41	$3,690
TLT4	Johnson	Penny	FL3497	209	$18,810
TLT5	Loyal	Jennifer	FL3497	351	$31,590
TLT5	Loyal	Jennifer	FL3602	65	$5,850
TLT5	Loyal	Jennifer	FL3498	196	$17,640
TLT6	Reynolds	Adam	EM1430	439	$35,120
TLT7	Garica	Karen	RL4408	83	$6,640
TLT7	Garica	Karen	RL4009	429	$34,320
TLT8	Li	Rob	WC6782	162	$12,150
TLT8	Li	Rob	WC5555	621	$46,575
TLT9	Tanaka	Hanne	WC5555	293	$21,975
TLT9	Tanaka	Hanne	WC6749	705	$52,875
TLT9	Tanaka	Hanne	PI5513	312	$23,400
Total					**$529,835**

Page 1

Access 2016, Windows 10, Microsoft Corporation.

FIGURE 4.15 Project 4E Caseload Database—Total Caseload Fees Query

17 Create a query as shown in Figure 4.15, using both tables.

- Use the fields **Staff ID**, **Last Name**, **First Name**, **Case Number**, and **Billable Hours**.
- Create a field **Caseload Fees** to calculate the caseload fees by multiplying the **Billing Rate** by the **Billable Hours**.
- Use criteria to only display the case fees if the **Billable Hours** are greater than zero.
- Sort by **Staff ID** in ascending order.
- Set the properties for **Caseload Fees** to *Currency* with zero decimal places.
- Run the query. At the bottom of the results, add a total row to total the **Caseload Fees**.
- Save the query as **Lastname_Firstname_4E_Total_Caseload_Fees**, and close the query.

(Project 4E Caseload Database continues on the next page)

PROJECT RESULTS

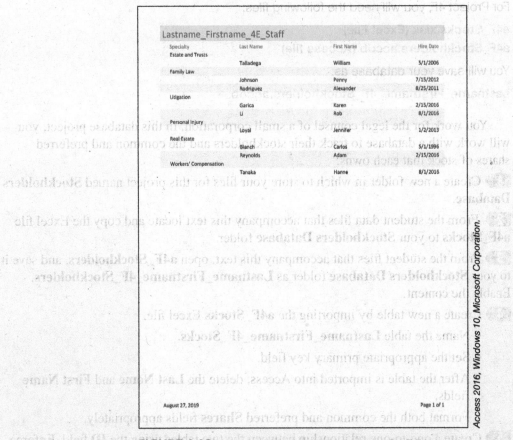

FIGURE 4.16 Project 4E Caseload Database—Staff Report

18 ▸ Using the Report Wizard, create a report as shown in Figure 4.16.

- Use **Last Name**, **First Name**, **Specialty**, and **Hire Date** from the **Lastname_Firstname_4E_Staff** table.
- Group by **Specialty**.
- Sort by **Last Name** in ascending order.
- Accept the *Stepped* and *Portrait* default settings.
- Finish the report, saving with the default name.
- Modify the report in Layout view. Resize and reposition columns so that all data is visible and evenly spaced. If necessary, reposition the page number in the footer.
- Save the report and close it.

19 ▸ Save the database, and submit it as directed by your instructor.

END | You have completed Project 4E

OUTCOMES-BASED ASSESSMENTS

Apply skills from these objectives:

1. Open and Save an Existing Database
2. Change the Structure of Tables and Add a Second Table
3. Create Table Relationships
4. Create a Query in Query Design
5. Specify Criteria in a Query
6. Specify Numeric Criteria in a Query
7. Use Compound Criteria
8. Create a Query Based on More Than One Table
9. Create Calculated Fields in a Query
10. Create and Use a Form to Add Records
11. Create a Report Using the Report Wizard
12. Modify the Design of a Report
13. Close a Database and Exit Access

GO! Think   Project 4F Stockholders Database

 PROJECT FILES

For Project 4F, you will need the following files:

a4F_Stocks.xlsx (Excel File)

a4F_Stockholders.accdb (Access file)

You will save your database as:

Lastname_Firstname_4F_Stockholders.accdb

You work for the legal counsel of a small corporation. In this database project, you will work with a database to track their stockholders and the common and preferred shares of stock that each owns.

1 Create a new folder in which to store your files for this project named **Stockholders Database**.

2 From the student data files that accompany this text locate and copy the Excel file **a4F_Stocks** to your **Stockholders Database** folder.

3 From the student files that accompany this text, open **a4F_Stockholders**, and save it to your **Stockholders Database** folder as **Lastname_Firstname_4F_Stockholders**. Enable the content.

4 Create a new table by importing the **a4F_Stocks** Excel file.

- Name the table **Lastname_Firstname_4F_Stocks.**
- Set the appropriate primary key field.
- After the table is imported into Access, delete the **Last Name** and **First Name** fields.
- Format both the common and preferred **Shares** fields appropriately.

5 Create a one-to-one relationship between the two tables using the **ID** field. Enforce referential integrity.

6 Create a form for the **4F Stockholders** table, and accept the default name. Use the form to add the following two new stockholders.

ID: 13-1876	ID: 13-1877
Marta Washington	Wally Asterisk
2899 West Colorado	1735 Big Oak Drive
Colorado Springs, CO 80903	Colorado Springs, CO 80919
Call me during the day? Yes	Call me during the day? No
Day phone: 719-555-5534	Day phone: 719-555-2389
Call me in the evening? No	Call me in the evening? Yes
Evening phone: 719-555-2234	Evening phone: 719-555-3899
E-mail me? Yes	E-mail me? Yes
E-mail address: mwashing2@url.com	E-mail address: asteriskwa@url.com

(Project 4F Stockholders Database continues on the next page)

OUTCOMES-BASED ASSESSMENTS

7 Create a form for the **Lastname Firstname 4F Stocks** table, and accept the default name. Add the following two new records to the table.

ID: 13-1876	ID: 13-1877
Common Shares: 182000	Common Shares: 125000
Series A Preferred Shares: 0	Series A Preferred Shares: 0

8 Create the following queries. Show all pertinent fields. Sort appropriately. Save with descriptive names.

- Create a query that answers the question, *Which stockholder has both common stock and series A preferred stock greater than zero?*
- Create a query that answers the question, *What are the names and phone numbers of the stockholders who prefer to be called anytime?*
- Create a query that answers the question, *Which stockholders have zero common shares?*
- Create a query that answers the question, *Which stockholders have series A preferred stock >25,000?*
- To answer the questions *What is the total number of common shares?* and *What is the total number of series A preferred shares?*, create a query and then add a total row to the bottom of the results. Format number fields appropriately.
- Create a query using both tables to answer the question, *What is the total number of both kinds of shares that each stockholder owns?* Create a calculated field **Total Shares** that shows the total **Common Shares** and **Series A Preferred Shares**. Format number fields appropriately. Add a total row after running the query to SUM each number column.

9 Create a report based on the query you just made. Modify the report in Layout view, and then ensure that the columns are evenly spaced on the page and all information is visible. Save and close the report.

10 Close the database, and submit it as directed by your instructor.

END | You have completed Project 4F

CONTENT-BASED ASSESSMENTS

Apply skills from these objectives:

1 Edit a Presentation in Normal View
2 Edit an Existing Presentation
3 Add Pictures to a Presentation
4 Print and View a Presentation
5 Format Slides
6 Apply Slide Transitions
7 Insert Text Boxes and Shapes
8 Format Objects
9 Remove Picture Backgrounds and Insert WordArt
10 Create and Format a SmartArt Graphic
11 Customize Slide Backgrounds and Themes
12 Animate a Slide Show
13 Create and Modify Tables
14 Create and Modify Charts

 PROJECT FILES

For Project 4G, you will need the following files:

p4G_Jury_Selection.pptx
p4G_Jury_Qualifications.pptx
p4G_Federal_Court.jpg
p4G_Courtroom.jpg

You will save your presentation as:

Lastname_Firstname_4G_Jury_Selection

(Project 4G Jury Selection continues on the next page)

PROJECT RESULTS

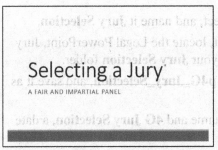

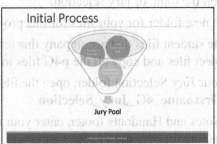

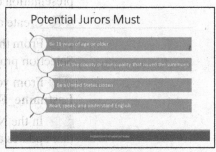

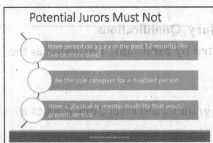

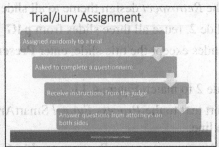

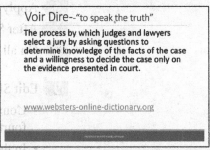

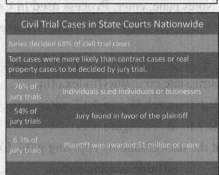

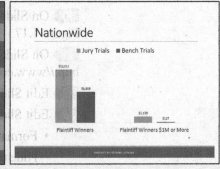

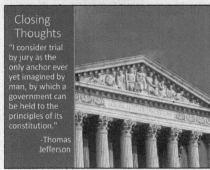

FIGURE 4.17 Project 4G Jury Selection

PowerPoint 2016, Windows 10, Microsoft Corporation.

(Project 4G Jury Selection continues on the next page)

1 As an intern at a large law firm, you have been asked to prepare a short training presentation on the topic of jury selection.

2 Create a new folder for your files for this project, and name it **Jury Selection**.

3 From the student files that accompany this text, locate the Legal PowerPoint, Jury Selection project files and copy all the **p4G** files to your **Jury Selection** folder.

4 From your Jury Selection folder, open the file **p4G_Jury_Selection**, and save it as **Lastname_Firstname_4G_Jury_Selection**.

5 In the Notes and Handouts footer, enter your name and **4G Jury Selection**, a date that updates automatically, and the page number.

6 Apply the *Retrospect* design theme to all slides.

7 After Slide 2, reuse all three slides from **p4G_Jury_Qualifications**.

8 On all slides except the title slide, enter **Presented by Firstname Lastname** as the footer.

9 Edit Slide 2 to match Figure 4.17:

- Convert text to the *Process Funnel* SmartArt graphic, and enter **Jury Pool** as a fourth line.
- In the Notes pane, enter: **Process used in Colorado. Other states may differ.**

10 On Slide 3, convert the text to a Vertical Curved List SmartArt graphic to match Figure 4.17.

11 On Slide 4, in the Notes pane, type the source of your information http://www.courts.state.co.us/Jury/Index.cfm.

12 Edit Slide 6 to match Figure 4.17, enter www.websters-online-dictionary.org.

13 Edit Slide 7 to match Figure 4.17:

- Format the background by applying **p4G_Courtroom** as a picture fill.
- Hide the background graphics.
- To the title and text placeholders, apply Shape Fill colors. Resize and position them.

14 Edit Slide 8 to match Figure 4.17:

- Apply a table style.
- Size the table, and position it on the slide.
- Align the text, and set the font sizes.

15 Edit Slide 9 to match Figure 4.17:

- Change the slide title to **Nationwide**.
- Create a clustered column chart using the following data.

	Jury Trials	Bench Trials
Plaintiff Winners	$10,012	$5,809
Plaintiff Winners $1M or More	$1,159	$137

16 Edit Slide 10 to match Figure 4.17:

- Change the layout of the slide to Content with Caption.
- Insert the picture **p4G_Federal_Court**.

(Project 4G Jury Selection continues on the next page)

17 Apply the Doors transition to all slides.

18 Run the slide show and proofread.

19 Save the presentation, and submit it as directed by your instructor.

END | You have completed Project 4G

OUTCOMES-BASED ASSESSMENTS

Apply skills from these objectives:

1 Create a New Presentation
2 Edit a Presentation in Normal View
3 Add Pictures to a Presentation
4 Print and View a Presentation
5 Format Slides
6 Apply Slide Transitions
7 Format Numbered and Bulleted Lists
8 Insert Online Pictures
9 Create and Format a SmartArt Graphic
10 Animate a Slide Show
11 Create and Modify Tables
12 Create and Modify Charts

 PROJECT FILES

For Project 4H, you will need the following file:

New blank PowerPoint presentation

You will save your presentation as:

Lastname_Firstname_4H_Community

Your local legal professional organization does community service workshops on legal topics. You have volunteered to create the presentation for next month.

1 Create a new folder to store your files for this project, and name the folder **Community**.

2 Create and save a new presentation file in your **Community** folder with the name **Lastname_Firstname_4H_Community**.

3 Find information related to a topic that you think would be of interest to those in your local community. Examples include information about appointment of a guardian, appointment of a conservator, bankruptcy, estates, evictions, victim restitution, probate, or small claims. Cite your source(s) in your presentation.

4 Enter **Lastname Firstname 4H Community** as a Notes and Handouts footer.

5 Apply an appropriate design theme. Customize the background or theme.

6 Try to follow the 6 × 6 rule on slides with bulleted lists. (No more than six lines of text and no more than six words in a line.)

7 Use at least one table *or* chart.

8 Insert an online picture or a photo.

9 Enter notes in the Notes pane of points you plan to make during the presentation.

10 Apply slide transitions.

11 Run the slide show and proofread.

12 Save the presentation, and submit it as directed by your instructor.

END | You have completed Project 4H

Proper Business Letter Format

There is a specific format required for a one-page business letter. Use the following instructions, and use Figure A as a model to create your own properly formatted business letter.

1 ▶ Starting with a blank document, set the text style to **No Spacing**.

2 ▶ Set 1" left, right, and bottom margins. Set a top margin of .5".

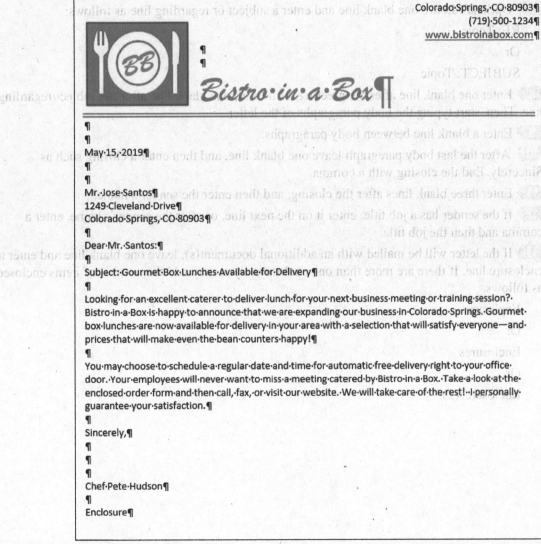

FIGURE A

Word 2016, Windows 10, Microsoft Corporation.

3 Enter and format the **letterhead**, including the sender's company name, address, perhaps a logo, and other contact information. Do not type the letterhead in the header of the document. The majority of business letters are limited to one page.

If a letter is too long to fit on one page, the additional page(s) should not have a letterhead at the top. No heading or letterhead is required on the second page, especially if printed on the back of the same piece of paper. At the top of additional pages, you may enter the recipient's title (i.e., Mr., Ms., Miss, or Professor); first and last name; the page number; and the date of the letter—type the name of the month. Complete the rest of the letter, using one plain font, font size 10–12 pt, all left aligned, and with no indenting or tabs at the start of paragraphs.

4 Enter two blank lines after the letterhead, and then enter the **date**. Type out the name of the month.

5 Enter three blank lines after the date, and then enter the recipient's name and address as follows, pressing Enter at the end of each line:

Title FirstnameLastname   *(Title examples: Mr., Ms., Miss, or Professor)*

999 Street

City, State postal#

6 Enter one blank line after the address, and then enter the title and **only the last name** in the greeting. End the greeting with a colon.

7 Optional: Leave one blank line and enter a subject or regarding line as follows:

RE: Topic

Or

SUBJECT: Topic

8 Enter one blank line after the greeting, or if used, one blank line after the subject/regarding line. Then, start typing the body paragraphs of the letter.

9 Enter a blank line between body paragraphs.

10 After the last body paragraph leave one blank line, and then enter a closing such as Sincerely. End the closing with a comma.

11 Enter three blank lines after the closing, and then enter the sender's name.

12 If the sender has a job title, enter it on the next line, or after the sender's name, enter a comma and then the job title.

13 If the letter will be mailed with an additional document(s), leave one blank line and enter an enclosure line. If there are more than one enclosures, you may add the number of items enclosed, as follows:

Enclosure

Or

Enclosures

Or

Enclosures(2)

Basic MLA Paper Formatting with Microsoft Word 2016

Many college professors want papers to be typed in MLA format. Start Word, and do the following:

1 Set Double Spacing.

- First, start with a blank document or select all of your existing text.
- Set the text style to **No Spacing**.
- Set the **Line Spacing** to **2**.

2 Set the Font for the Entire Document.

- Set the font to **Times New Roman** (your instructor may accept another plain font).
- Set the font size to **12 pt**.

3 Insert Page Numbering.

- On the **Insert tab**, click **Page Number**.
- Click **Top of Page, Plain Number 3**.
- Enter your **last name**, leaving a space before the page number.
- Be sure your name and page number are **Times New Roman, 12 pt**.
- **Close** the header.

4 Enter the MLA Paper Heading.

- On the **References tab**, click the **MLA Citations & Bibliography Style**.
- Type **your name**, and then press Enter.
- Type your **instructor's name**, and then press Enter.
- Type the **class**, and then press Enter.
- Type the **date**, and then press Enter.
- Click the **Center** align button.
- Type the **title** of your essay. Capitalize the first letter of each main word, and do not use underline, bold, or quotes. Press Enter.

5 Set the Margins.

Be sure the margins are set to 1" on all sides. If they are not:

- On the **Page Layout tab**, click **Margins**.
- Click **Normal**.

6 Save the Document.

- On the **File tab**, click **Save As**.
- Navigate to the location where you want to save the file. Pay careful attention to where you save and the name you give your file so that you can find it later.
- Click **Save**.

7 Enter Sources.

You must enter complete information for each book, journal article, webpage, or other source.

- On the **References tab**, in the **Citations & Bibliography group**, select **Manage Sources**.
- Click the **New** button.
- Select the **Show All Bibliography Fields** check box.
- Click the arrow next to **Type of source**, and click the best option.
- Enter the author's last name, a comma, and then the author's first name. (If there is no named author, select the **Corporate Author** check box, and then enter the organization that has provided the source information.)
- Carefully enter all the information you can about your source. Use proper capitalization and punctuation. Click the **OK** button.

8 Type the Body of the Paper.

Be very careful to use your own words, phrases, and sentence constructions to avoid plagiarism.

- Click the **Left** align button.
- **Tab** .5" to start each paragraph. Do not leave extra spacing between paragraphs.
- **Save** every five to ten minutes as you compose your paper.

9 Enter Parenthetical References.

In the body of the paper, each time you paraphrase or quote a source, you must enter a reference. Either mention the author's last name in the body text and then put only the page number, if there is one, in parentheses at the end of the paraphrased material or put both the author's last name and the page number, if there is one, in parentheses. Put no comma in the parentheses.

- Click after the text to cite.
- On the **References tab**, in the **Citations & Bibliography group**, click **Insert Citation**, and then select the appropriate source from the list.
- Right-click the citation, select **Edit Citation**, and then enter the page number(s) and suppress the author's name if it is already mentioned in your text.

10 Create the Works Cited Page.

- Use Ctrl + Enter to start a new page.
- On the **References tab**, in the **Citations & Bibliography group**, click **Bibliography**, then scroll down and click **Works Cited**.
- Format the text on the Works Cited pages as Black, 12 pt size, Times New Roman font. Double-space the paragraphs, and ensure that there is no spacing added before or after the paragraphs.
- Center the title **Works Cited**. Remove the bold formatting, if necessary.
- Verify that all the data for the sources display accurately. Make any fixes needed in the Source Manager.

11 ▶ **Complete the Paper.**

- On the **Review tab**, click **Spelling & Grammar** to check the document.
- Proofread the entire paper, and then **Save** the document.
- If your instructor does not have Office 2016, on the **File tab**, click **Save As**, and then navigate to where you are saving your files.
- In the **Save as type** box, click **Rich Text Format (RTF)**.
- Pay careful attention to where you save and the name you give your file so that you can find it when you must upload it or print it later.
- Click **Save**.

For more detailed information and examples, consult the authoritative and complete *MLA Handbook for Writers of Research Papers* (8th edition), www.mlahandbook.org. Or see an excellent style guide at *The Purdue OWL*. Purdue U Writing Lab, http://owl.english.purdue.edu/owl.

Tracking Changes in Word Documents

Microsoft Word's Track Changes feature is used in **Client Mailing Project 4A, Part 2 Motion Testimony**. Track Changes is a Word feature that enables you to view revisions to a document and insert comments. This is useful when making proposed changes to a document that will later be reviewed by you or others. The changes can be either accepted or rejected. Changes to legal documents are often tracked in this way. For example, a contract might be reviewed by an attorney who will recommend changes. If the changes to the electronic document are tracked, both the original text and the recommended text can be viewed for easy comparison. You can accept or reject changes individually, or you can accept or reject all changes in a document at once.

To track changes while you edit, follow these steps to turn on Track Changes:

1. Open the document that you want to revise.

2. On the **Review tab**, in the **Tracking group**, click the **Track Changes** button. As you edit the document, the text will be marked with a specific color, underline, or strikethrough, as shown in Figure C.1.

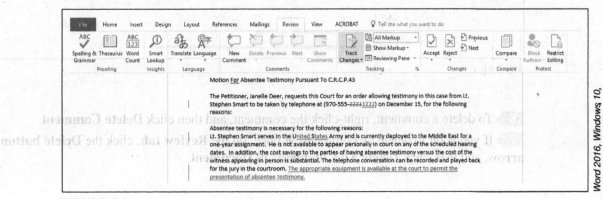

FIGURE C.1

3. Comments may also be inserted. To insert a comment, position the insertion point at the desired text (or select the text), and then on the **Review tab**, in the **Comments group**, click the **New Comment** button. Type the text for the comment.

4. To turn off the tracking feature, click the **Track Changes** button again.

To view changes tracked in a document:

1. Open the document you want to review.

2. On the **Review tab**, in the **Tracking group**, click the **Show Markup arrow** to select how the changes are displayed. The **Show Markup** menu will allow you to customize the way the tracking elements display in your document.

To display the Reviewing Pane, follow these steps:

1 Another way to view tracked changes is to display the **Reviewing Pane**. On the **Review tab**, in the **Tracking group**, click the down arrow to the right of **Reviewing Pane**.

2 Click **Reviewing Pane Vertical**.

3 When the Reviewing Pane is no longer needed, close the pane by repeating these steps or by clicking the **Close** button in the top right corner of the pane.

To view and accept or reject changes, follow these steps:

1 Open the document you want to review. Place the insertion point at the beginning of the document or at the location where you will begin reviewing changes.

2 Click the **Track Changes** button to turn off the feature if it is active.

3 On the **Review tab**, in the **Changes group**, click **Next** to move to the first change.

4 On the **Review tab**, in the **Changes group**, click the **Accept** button if you want to accept the change. If you want to reject the change, click the **Reject** button. After you accept or reject a change, Word will move on to the next change automatically.

5 If you want to accept all of the changes at once, on the **Review tab**, click the **Accept button arrow**, and then click **Accept All Changes**. If you want to reject all changes at once, click the **Reject button arrow**, and then click **Reject All Changes** (see Figure C.2).

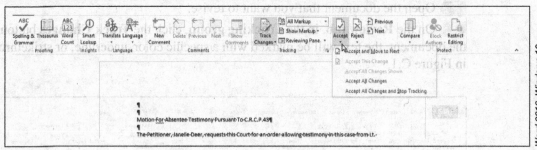

Word 2016, Windows 10, Microsoft Corporation.

FIGURE C.2

6 To delete a comment, right-click the comment, and then click **Delete Comment**.

7 If you want to delete all comments at once, on the **Review tab**, click the **Delete button arrow**, and then click **Delete All Comments in Document**.

Index

A

Access
Billing Database Project, 65–66
Caseload Database Project, 127–137
Community Policing Database Project, 99
Inventory Database Project, 55–64
Kitchen Inventory Database Project, 28–29
Recipe Database Project, 20–27
Stockholders Database Project, 138–139
Training Database Project, 90–98
Administration of justice
Community Policing Database Project, 99
Community Presentation Project, 103
Cyber Crime Presentation Project, 100–102
Neighborhood Watch Mailing Project, 72–79
Parking Project, 88–89
Police Calls Project, 84–87
Seniors Mailing Project, 80–83
Training Database Project, 90–98

B

Billable Hours Project, 125–126
Billing Database Project, 65–66

C

Caseload Database Project, 127–137
Client Mailing Project, 106–114
Client Letter, 106–107
Form Letters, 113–114
Labels, 111–112
Motion Testimony, 108–110
Community Garden Presentation Project, 30–32
Community Policing Database Project, 99
Community Presentation Project, 144
Community Presentation Project, 103
Culinary Arts, 2–33
Community Garden Presentation Project, 30–32
Culinary Bistro Mailing Project, 2–9
Culinary Gala Mailing Project, 10–13
Food Costing Project, 14–17
Healthy Recipe Presentation Project, 33
Hudson Grill Project, 18–19
Kitchen Inventory Database Project, 28–29
Recipe Database Project, 20–27
Culinary Bistro Mailing Project, 2-9
Bistro Flyer, 4–5
Bistro Letter, 2–3
Form Letters, 8–9
Labels, 6–7
Culinary Gala Mailing Project, 10–13
Form Letters, 13
Gala Flyer, 11
Gala Letter, 10
Labels, 12
Cyber Crime Presentation Project, 100–102

E

Excel
Billable Hours Project, 125–126
Food Costing Project, 14–17
Hudson Grill Project, 18–19
Medical Invoice Project, 49–52
Medical Supplies Order Project, 53–54
Parking Project, 88–89
Police Calls Project, 84–87
Stockholder Ledger Project, 120–124

F

Food Costing Project, 14–17
Form Letters
Client Mailing Project, 113–114
Culinary Bistro Mailing Project, 8–9
Culinary Gala Mailing Project, 13
Healthcare Dental Mailing Project, 42–43
Healthcare Medical Mailing Project, 48
Legal Stock Mailing Project, 119
Neighborhood Watch Mailing Project, 78–79
Seniors Mailing Project, 83

H

Healthcare
Billing Database Project, 65–66
Healthcare Dental Mailing Project, 36–43
Healthcare Medical Mailing Project, 44–48
Inventory Database Project, 55–64
Lowering Blood Pressure Presentation Project, 67–69
Medical Invoice Project, 49–52
Medical Supplies Order Project, 53–54
Patient Presentation Project, 70
Healthcare Dental Mailing Project, 36–43
Dental Letter, 36–37
Dental Newsletter, 38–39
Form Letters, 42–43
Labels, 40–41
Healthcare Medical Mailing Project, 44–48
Form Letters, 48
Labels, 47
Medical Letter, 44
MLA Paper, 45–46
Healthy Recipe Presentation Project, 33
Hudson Grill Project, 18–19

I

Inventory Database Project, 55–64

J

Jury Selection Project, 140–143

K

Kitchen Inventory Database Project, 28–29

L

Labels

Client Mailing Project, 111–112

Culinary Bistro Mailing, 6–7

Culinary Gala Mailing, 12

Healthcare Dental Mailing, 40–41

Healthcare Medical Mailing, 47

Legal Stock Mailing Project, 118

Neighborhood Watch Mailing, 76–77

Seniors Mailing, 82

Legal projects

Billable Hours Project, 125–126

Caseload Database Project, 127–137

Client Mailing Project, 106–114

Community Presentation Project, 144

Jury Selection Project, 140–143

Legal Stock Mailing Project, 115–119

Stockholder Ledger Project, 120–124

Stockholders Database Project, 138–139

Legal Stock Mailing Project, 115–119

Copyright Law Paper, 116–117

Form Letters, 119

Labels, 118

Stock Letter, 115

Lowering Blood Pressure Presentation Project, 67–69

M

Medical Invoice Project, 49–52

Medical Supplies Order Project, 53–54

N

Neighborhood Watch Mailing Project, 72–79

Form Letters, 78–79

Labels, 76–77

Newsletter, 74–75

Watch Letter, 72–73

P

Parking Project, 88–89

Patient Presentation Project, 70

Police Calls Project, 84–87

PowerPoint

Community Garden Presentation Project, 30–32

Community Presentation Project, 144

Community Presentation Project, 103

Cyber Crime Presentation Project, 100–102

Healthy Recipe Presentation Project, 33

Jury Selection Project, 140–143

Lowering Blood Pressure Presentation Project, 67–69

Patient Presentation Project, 70

R

Recipe Database Project, 20–27

S

Seniors Mailing Project, 80–83

Form Letters, 83

Labels, 82

Newsletter, 81

Seniors Letter, 80

Stockholder Ledger Project, 120–124

Stockholders Database Project, 138–139

T

Training Database Project, 90–98

W

Word

Client Mailing Project, 106–114

Culinary Bistro Mailing Project, 2–9

Culinary Gala Mailing Project, 10–13

Healthcare Dental Mailing Project, 36–43

Healthcare Medical Mailing Project, 44–48

Legal Stock Mailing Project, 115–119

Neighborhood Watch Mailing Project, 72–79

Seniors Mailing Project, 80–83